Revenue Recognition

Steven M. Bragg

AccountingTools®

ISBN-13: 978-1-64221-295-2

For more information about AccountingTools® products, visit our Web site at www.accountingtools.com.

Table of Contents

Chapter 1
Revenue Recognition

Introduction

Historically, the accounting standards related to the recognition of revenue have built up in a piecemeal manner, with guidance being established separately for certain industries and types of transactions. The result has been an inconsistent set of standards that, while workable, have not resulted in revenue recognition principles that could be applied consistently across many industries.

The accounting for revenue has been streamlined to a considerable extent with the release of Topic 606 in Generally Accepted Accounting Principles (GAAP), which is essentially duplicated in the International Financial Reporting Standards (IFRS). Now, the overall intent of revenue recognition is to do so in a manner that reasonably depicts the transfer of goods or services to customers, for which consideration is paid that reflects the amount to which the seller expects to be entitled. The following sections describe the five-step process of revenue recognition, as well as a number of ancillary topics.

> **Related Podcast Episodes:** Episodes 179 and 205 of the Accounting Best Practices Podcast discuss revenue recognition. They are available at: **accounting-tools.com/podcasts** or **iTunes**

Topic 606, Revenue from Contracts with Customers

The most comprehensive accounting standard to date that deals with revenue recognition is Topic 606 of the Accounting Standards Codification, *Revenue from Contracts with Customers*. This standard establishes a consistent framework for how to address revenue issues, while at the same time eliminating a number of inconsistencies in prior accounting standards relating to revenue. The result should be a higher level of comparability of revenue practices across multiple industries.

Topic 606 is now the overarching revenue standard, since it applies to any entity that contractually sells goods or services to customers. This accounting standard focuses on the overall principles guiding the recognition of revenue, rather than establishing a large number of detailed rules to govern the actions of accountants. The result is a topic that emphasizes the use of judgment in following general guidelines.

Topic 606 does not completely supplant the revenue-related guidance in other accounting standards. In cases where more detailed guidance is available in the accounting standards that deal with a transaction, the more detailed guidance should be applied rather than the guidance found in Topic 606.

The following sections delve into the essentials of *Revenue from Contracts with Customers*.

The Nature of a Customer

Revenue recognition only occurs if the third party involved is a customer. A customer is an entity that has contracted to obtain goods or services from the seller's ordinary activities in exchange for payment.

In some situations, it may require a complete examination of the facts and circumstances to determine whether the other party can be classified as a customer. For example, it can be difficult to discern whether there is a customer in collaborative research and development activities between pharmaceutical entities. Another difficult area is payments between oil and gas partners to settle differences between their entitlements to the output from a producing field.

EXAMPLE

The Red Herring Fish Company contracts with Lethal Sushi to co-develop a fish farm off the coast of Iceland, where the two entities share equally in any future profits. Lethal Sushi is primarily in the restaurant business, so developing a fish farm is not one of its ordinary activities. Also, there is no clear consideration being paid to Lethal. Based on the circumstances, Red Herring is not a customer of Lethal Sushi.

Steps in Revenue Recognition

Topic 606 establishes a series of actions that an entity takes to determine the amount and timing of revenue to be recognized. The main steps are:

1. Link the contract with a specific customer.
2. Note the performance obligations required by the contract.
3. Determine the price of the underlying transaction.
4. Match this price to the performance obligations through an allocation process.
5. Recognize revenue as the various obligations are fulfilled.

We will expand upon each of these steps in the following sections.

Step One: Link Contract to Customer

The contract is used as a central aspect of revenue recognition, because revenue recognition is closely associated with it. In many instances, revenue is recognized at multiple points in time over the duration of a contract, so linking contracts with revenue recognition provides a reasonable framework for establishing the timing and amounts of revenue recognition.

A contract only exists if there is an agreement between the parties that establishes enforceable rights and obligations. It is not necessary for an agreement to be in writing for it to be considered a contract. More specifically, a contract only exists if the following conditions are present:

- *Approval.* All parties to the contract have approved the document and substantially committed to its contents (based on all relevant facts and circumstances). The parties can be considered to be committed to a contract despite occasional lapses, such as not enforcing prompt payment or sometimes shipping late. Approval can be in writing or orally.
- *Rights.* The document clearly identifies the rights of the parties.
- *Payment.* The payment terms are clearly stated. It is acceptable to recognize revenue related to unpriced change orders if the seller expects that the price will be approved and the scope of work has been approved.
- *Substance.* The agreement has commercial substance; that is, the cash flows of the seller will change as a result of the contract, either in terms of their amount, timing, or risk of receipt. Otherwise, organizations could swap goods or services to artificially boost their revenue.
- *Probability.* It is probable that the organization will collect substantially all of the amount stated in the contract in exchange for the goods or services that it commits to provide to the other party. In this context, "probable" means "likely to occur." This evaluation is based on the customer's ability and intention to pay when due. The evaluation can incorporate a consideration of the past practice of the customer in question, or of the class of customers to which that customer belongs.

If these criteria are not initially met, the seller can continue to evaluate the situation to see if the criteria are met at a later date.

> **Note:** These criteria do not *have* to be re-evaluated at a later date, unless the seller notes a significant change in the relevant facts and circumstances.

EXAMPLE

Prickly Corporation has entered into an arrangement to sell a large quantity of rose thorns to Ambivalence Corporation, which manufactures a number of potions for the amateur witch brewing market. The contract specifies monthly deliveries over the course of the next year.

Prior to the first shipment, Prickly's collections manager learns through her contacts that Ambivalence has just lost its line of credit and has conducted a large layoff. It appears that the customer's ability to pay has deteriorated significantly, which calls into question the probability of collecting the amount stated in the contract. In this case, there may no longer be a contract for the purposes of revenue recognition.

EXAMPLE

Domicilio Corporation, which develops commercial real estate, enters into a contract with Cupertino Beanery to sell a building to Cupertino to be used as a coffee shop. This is Cupertino's first foray into the coffee shop business, having previously only been a distributor of coffee beans to shops within the region. Also, there are a massive number of coffee shops already established in the area.

Domicilio receives a $100,000 deposit from Cupertino when the contract is signed. The contract also states that Cupertino will pay Domicilio an additional $900,000 for the rest of the property over the next three years, with interest. This financing arrangement is nonrecourse, meaning that Domicilio can repossess the building in the event of default, but cannot obtain further cash from Cupertino. Cupertino expects to pay Domicilio from the cash flows to be generated by the coffee shop operation.

Domicilio's management concludes that it is not probable that Cupertino will pay the remaining contractual amount, since its source of funds is a high-risk venture in which Cupertino has no experience. In addition, the loan is nonrecourse, so Cupertino can easily walk away from the arrangement. Accordingly, Domicilio accounts for the initial deposit and future payments as a deposit liability, and continues to recognize the building asset. If it later becomes probable that Cupertino will pay the full contractual amount, Domicilio can then recognize revenue and an offsetting receivable.

Whether a contract exists can depend upon standard industry practice, or vary by legal jurisdiction, or even vary by business segment.

There may be instances in which the preceding criteria are not met, and yet the customer is paying consideration to the seller. If so, revenue can be recognized only when one or more of the following events has occurred:

- The contract has been terminated and the consideration received by the seller is not refundable; or
- The seller has no remaining obligations to the customer, substantially all of the consideration has been received, and the payment is not refundable; or
- The seller has transferred control of the goods or services, *and* has stopped transferring goods or services to the customer, *and* has no obligation to transfer additional goods or services, *and* the consideration received cannot be refunded.

These alternatives focus on whether the contract has been concluded in all respects. If so, there is little risk that any revenue recognized will be reversed in a later period, and so is a highly conservative approach to recognizing revenue.

If the seller receives consideration from a customer and the preceding conditions do not exist, then the payment is to be recorded as a liability until such time as the sale criteria have been met.

A contract is not considered to exist when each party to the contract has a unilateral right to terminate a contract that has not been performed, and without compensating the other party. An unperformed contract is one in which no goods or services have been transferred to the customer, nor has the seller received any consideration from the customer in exchange for any promised goods or services.

In certain situations, it can make sense to combine several contracts into one for the purposes of revenue recognition. For example, if there is a portfolio of contracts that have similar characteristics, and the entity expects that treating the portfolio as a single unit will have no appreciable impact on the financial statements, it is acceptable to combine the contracts for accounting purposes. This approach may be particularly valuable in industries where there are a large number of similar contracts, and where applying the model to each individual contract could be impractical.

> **Tip:** When accounting for a portfolio of contracts, adjust the accompanying estimates and assumptions to reflect the greater size of the portfolio.

If the seller enters into two or more contracts with a customer at approximately the same time, these contracts can be accounted for as a single contract if any of the following criteria are met:

- *Basis of negotiation.* The contracts were negotiated as a package, with the goal of attaining a single commercial objective.
- *Interlinking consideration.* The consideration that will be paid under the terms of one contract is dependent upon the price or performance noted in the other contract.
- *Performance obligation.* There is essentially one performance obligation inherent in the two contracts.

EXAMPLE

Domicilio Corporation enters into three contracts with Milford Sound to construct a concert arena. These contracts involve construction of the concrete building shell, installation of seating, and the construction of a staging system. The three contracts are all needed in order to arrive at a functioning concert arena. Final payment on all three contracts shall be made once the final customer (a local municipality) approves the entire project.

Domicilio should account for these contracts as a single contract, since they are all directed toward the same commercial goal, payment is dependent on all three contracts being completed, and the performance obligation is essentially the same for all of the contracts.

Step Two: Note Performance Obligations

A performance obligation is essentially the unit of account for the goods or services contractually promised to a customer. The performance obligations in the contract must be clearly identified. This is important in recognizing revenue, since revenue is considered to be recognizable when goods or services are transferred to the customer. Examples of goods and services are noted in the following table.

Examples of Goods and Services

Item Sold	Example of the Seller
Arranging for another party to transfer goods or services	Travel agent selling airline tickets
Asset construction on behalf of a customer	Building construction company
Grant of a license	Software company issuing licenses to use its software
Grant of options to purchase additional goods or services	Airline granting frequent flier points
Manufactured goods	Manufacturer
Performance of contractually-mandated tasks	Consultant
Readiness to provide goods or services as needed	Snow plow operator, alarm system monitoring
Resale of merchandise	Retailer
Resale of rights to goods or services	Selling a priority for a new-model car delivery
Rights to future goods or services that can be resold	Wholesaler gives additional services to retailer buying a particular product

There may also be an implicit promise to deliver goods or services that is not stated in a contract, as implied by the customary business practices of the seller. If there is a valid expectation by the customer to receive these implicitly-promised goods or services, they should be considered a performance obligation. Otherwise, the seller might recognize the entire transaction price as revenue when in fact there are still goods or services yet to be provided.

If there is no performance obligation, then there is no revenue to be recognized. For example, a company could continually build up its inventory through ongoing production activities, but just because it has more sellable assets does not mean that it can report an incremental increase in the revenue in its income statement. If such an activity-based revenue recognition model were allowed, organizations could increase their revenues simply by increasing their rate of activity.

If there is more than one good or service to be transferred under the contract terms, only break it out as a separate performance obligation if it is a distinct obligation or there are a series of transfers to the customer of a distinct good or service. In the latter case, a separate performance obligation is assumed if there is a consistent pattern of transfer to the customer.

The "distinct" label can be applied to a good or service only if it meets both of the following criteria:

- *Capable of being distinct.* The customer can benefit from the good or service as delivered, or in combination with other resources that the customer can readily find; and

- *Distinct within the context of the contract.* The promised delivery of the good or service is separately identified within the contract.

Goods or services are more likely to be considered distinct when:

- The seller does not use the goods or services as a component of an integrated bundle of goods or services.
- The items do not significantly modify any other goods or services listed in the contract.
- The items are not highly interrelated with other goods or services listed in the contract.

The intent of these evaluative factors is to place a focus on how to determine whether goods or services are truly distinct within a contract. There is no need to assess the customer's intended use of any goods or services when making this determination.

To reduce the cost of noting performance obligations, it is not necessary to assess whether promised goods or services are performance obligations if they are immaterial in the context of the contract with the customer.

EXAMPLE

Aphelion Corporation sells a package of goods and services to Nova Corporation. The goods include a deep field telescope, an observatory to house the telescope, and calibration services for the telescope.

The observatory building can be considered distinct from the telescope and calibration services, because Nova could have the telescope installed in an existing facility instead. However, the telescope and calibration services are linked, since the telescope will not function properly unless it has been properly calibrated. Thus, one performance obligation can be considered the observatory, while the telescope and associated calibration can be stated as a separate obligation.

EXAMPLE

Norrona Software enters into a contract with a Scandinavian clothing manufacturer to transfer a software license for its clothing design software. The contract also states that Norrona will install the software and provide technical support for a two-year period. The installation process involves adjusting the data entry screens to match the needs of the clothing designers who will use the software. The software can be used without these installation changes. The technical support assistance is intended to provide advice to users regarding advanced features, and is not considered a key requirement for software users.

Since the software is functional without the installation process or the technical support, Norrona concludes that the items are not highly interrelated. Since these goods and services are distinct, the company should identify separate performance obligations for the software license, installation work, and technical support.

In the event that a good or service is not classified as distinct, aggregate it with other goods or services promised in the contract, until such time as a cluster of goods or services have been accumulated that can be considered distinct.

> **Note:** If a different GAAP topic describes how to separate out the elements of a contract or initially measure it, follow that guidance before the requirements of Topic 606.

An organization can elect to create an accounting policy to account for shipping and handling activities occurring after a customer has gained control of a good, to designate these activities as fulfilling the promise to transfer the good, rather than as an additional promised service. Doing so reduces the complexity of accounting for the overall transaction.

The administrative tasks needed to fulfill a contract are not considered to be performance obligations, since they do not involve the transfer of goods or services to customers. For example, setting up information about a new contract in the seller's contract management software is not considered a performance obligation.

Step Three: Determine Prices

This step involves the determination of the transaction price built into the contract. The transaction price is the amount of consideration to be paid by the customer in exchange for its receipt of goods or services. The transaction price does not include any amounts collected on behalf of third parties (such as sales taxes).

EXAMPLE

The Twister Vacuum Company sells its vacuum cleaners to individuals through its chain of retail stores. In the most recent period, Twister generated $3,800,000 of receipts, of which $200,000 was sales taxes collected on behalf of local governments. Since the $200,000 was collected on behalf of third parties, it cannot be recognized as revenue.

The transaction price may be difficult to determine, since it involves consideration of the effects noted in the following subsections.

Variable Consideration

The terms of some contracts may result in a price that can vary, depending on the circumstances. For example, there may be discounts, rebates, penalties, or performance bonuses in the contract. Or, the customer may have a reasonable expectation that the seller will offer a price concession, based on the seller's customary business practices, policies, or statements. Another example is when the seller intends to accept lower prices from a new customer in order to develop a strong customer relationship. If so, set the transaction price based on either the most likely amount or the probability-weighted expected value, using whichever method yields that amount of consideration most likely to be paid.

In more detail, these methods are:

- *Most likely.* The seller develops a range of possible payment amounts, and selects the amount most likely to be paid. This approach works best when there are only two possible amounts that will be paid.
- *Expected value.* The seller develops a range of possible payment amounts, and assigns a probability to each one. The sum of these probability-weighted amounts is the expected value of the variable consideration. This approach works best when there are a large number of possible payment amounts. However, the outcome may be an expected value that does not exactly align with any amount that could actually be paid.

EXAMPLE

Grissom Granaries operates grain storage facilities along the Mississippi River. Its accounting staff is reviewing a contract that has just been signed with a major farming co-operative, and concludes that the contract could have four possible outcomes, which are noted in the following expected value table:

Price Scenario	Transaction Price	Probability	Probability-Weighted Price
1	$1,500,000	20%	$300,000
2	1,700,000	35%	595,000
3	2,000,000	40%	800,000
4	2,400,000	5%	120,000
		Expected Value	$1,815,000

The expected value derived from the four possible pricing outcomes is $1,815,000, even though this amount does not match any one of the four pricing outcomes.

Whichever method is chosen, be sure to use it consistently throughout the contract, as well as for similar contracts. However, it is not necessary to use the same measurement method to measure each uncertainty contained within a contract; different methods can be applied to different uncertainties.

Also, review the circumstances of each contract at the end of each reporting period, and update the estimated transaction price to reflect any changes in the circumstances.

EXAMPLE

Cantilever Construction has entered into a contract to tear down and replace five bridges along Interstate 70. The state government (which owns and maintains this section of the highway) is extremely concerned about how the work will interfere with traffic on the highway. Accordingly, the government includes in the contract a clause that penalizes Cantilever $10,000 for every hour over the budgeted amount that each bridge demolition and construction project shuts down the interstate, and a $15,000 bonus for every hour saved from the budgeted amount.

Cantilever has extensive experience with this type of work, having torn down and replaced 42 other bridges along the interstate highway system in the past five years. Based on the company's experience with these other projects and an examination of the budgeted hours allowed for shutting down the interstate, the company concludes that the most likely outcome is $120,000 of variable consideration associated with the project. Cantilever accordingly adds this amount to the transaction price.

Possibility of Reversal

Do not include in the transaction price an estimate of variable consideration if, when the uncertainty associated with the variable amount is settled, it is probable that there will be a significant reversal of cumulative revenue recognized. The assessment of a possible reversal of revenue could include the following factors, all of which might increase the probability of a revenue reversal:

- *Beyond seller's influence.* The amount of consideration paid is strongly influenced by factors outside of the control of the seller. For example, goods sold may be subject to obsolescence (as is common in the technology industry), or weather conditions could impede the availability of goods (as is common in the production of farm products).
- *Historical practice.* The seller has a history of accepting a broad range of price concessions, or of changing the terms of similar contracts.
- *Inherent range of outcomes.* The terms of the contract contain a broad range of possible consideration amounts that might be paid.
- *Limited experience.* The seller does not have much experience with the type of contract in question. Alternatively, the seller's prior experience cannot be translated into a prediction of the amount of consideration paid.
- *Long duration.* A considerable period of time may have to pass before the uncertainty can be resolved.

> **Note:** The probability of a significant reversal of cumulative revenue recognized places a conservative bias on the recognition of revenue, rather than a neutral bias, so there will be a tendency for recognized revenue levels to initially be too low. However, this approach is reasonable when considering that revenue information is more relevant when it is not subject to future reversals.

If management expects that a retroactive discount will be applied to sales transactions, the seller should recognize a refund liability as part of the revenue recognition when each performance obligation is satisfied. For example, if the seller is currently selling goods for $100 but expects that a 20% volume discount will be retroactively applied at the end of the year, the resulting entry should be:

	Debit	Credit
Accounts receivable	100	
Revenue		80
Refund liability		20

EXAMPLE

Medusa Medical sells a well-known snake oil therapy through a number of retail store customers. In the most recent month, Medusa sells $100,000 of its potent Copperhead Plus combination healing balm and sunscreen lotion. The therapy is most effective within one month of manufacture and then degrades rapidly, so that Medusa must accept increasingly large price concessions in order to ensure that the goods are sold. Historically, this means that the range of price concessions varies from zero (in the first month) to 80% (after four months). Of this range of outcomes, Medusa estimates that the expected value of the transactions is likely to be revenue of $65,000. However, since the risk of obsolescence is so high, Medusa cannot conclude that it is probable that there will not be a significant reversal in the amount of cumulative revenue recognized. Accordingly, management concludes that the price point at which it is probable that there will not be a significant reversal in the cumulative amount of revenue recognized is actually closer to $45,000 (representing a 55% price concession). Based on this conclusion, the controller initially recognizes $45,000 of revenue when the goods are shipped to retailers, and continues to monitor the situation at the end of each reporting period, to see if the recognized amount should be adjusted.

EXAMPLE

Iceland Cod enters into a contract with Lethal Sushi to provide Lethal with 10,000 pounds of cod per year, at $15 per pound. If Lethal purchases more than 10,000 pounds within one calendar year, then a 12% retroactive price reduction will be applied to all of Lethal's purchases for the year.

Iceland has dealt with Lethal for a number of years, and knows that Lethal has never attained the 10,000 pound level of purchases. Accordingly, through the first half of the year, Iceland records its sales to Lethal at their full price, which is $30,000 for 2,000 pounds of cod.

In July, Lethal acquires Wimpy Fish Company, along with its large chain of seafood restaurants. With a much larger need for fish to supply the additional restaurants, Lethal now places several large orders that make it quite clear that passing the 10,000 pound threshold will be no problem at all. Accordingly, Iceland's controller records a cumulative revenue reversal of $3,600 to account for Lethal's probable attainment of the volume purchase discount.

EXAMPLE

Armadillo Industries is a new company that has developed a unique type of ceramic-based body armor that is extremely light. To encourage sales, the company is offering a 90-day money back guarantee. Since the company is new to the industry and cannot predict the level of returns, there is no way of knowing if a sudden influx of returns might trigger a significant reversal in the amount of cumulative revenue recognized. Accordingly, the company must wait for the money back guarantee to expire before it can recognize any revenue.

Time Value of Money

If the transaction price is to be paid over a period of time, this implies that the seller is including a financing component in the contract. If this financing component is a significant financing benefit for the customer and provides financing for more than one year, adjust the transaction price for the time value of money. In cases where there is a financing component to a contract, the seller will earn interest income over the term of the contract.

A contract may contain a financing component, even if there is no explicit reference to it in the contract. When adjusting the transaction price for the time value of money, consider the following factors:

- *Standalone price.* The amount of revenue recognized should reflect the price that a customer would have paid if it had paid in cash.
- *Significance.* In order to be recognized, the financing component should be significant. This means evaluating the amount of the difference between the consideration to be paid and the cash selling price. Also note the combined effect of prevailing interest rates and the time difference between when delivery is made and when the customer pays.

If it is necessary to adjust the compensation paid for the time value of money, use as a discount rate the rate that would be employed in a separate financing transaction between the parties as of the beginning date of the contract. The rate used should reflect the credit characteristics of the customer, including the presence of any collateral provided. This discount rate is not to be updated after the commencement of the contract, irrespective of any changes in the credit markets or in the credit standing of the customer.

EXAMPLE

Hammer Industries sells a large piece of construction equipment to Eskimo Construction, under generous terms that allow Eskimo to pay Hammer the full amount of the $119,990 receivable in 24 months. The cash selling price of the equipment is $105,000. The contract contains an implicit interest rate of 6.9%, which is the interest rate that discounts the purchase price of $119,990 down to the cash selling price over the two year period. The controller examines this rate and concludes that it approximates the rate that Hammer and Eskimo would use if there had been a separate financing transaction between them as of the contract inception date.

Consequently, Hammer recognizes interest income during the two-year period prior to the payment due date, using the following calculation:

Year	Beginning Balance	Interest (at 6.9% Rate)	Ending Balance
1	$105,000	$7,245	$112,245
2	112,245	7,745	$119,990

As of the shipment date, Hammer records the following entry:

	Debit	Credit
Loan receivable	105,000	
Revenue		105,000

At the end of the first year, Hammer recognizes the interest associated with the transaction for the first year, using the following entry:

	Debit	Credit
Loan receivable	7,245	
Interest income		7,245

At the end of the second year, Hammer recognizes the interest associated with the transaction for the second year, using the following entry:

	Debit	Credit
Loan receivable	7,745	
Interest income		7,745

These entries increase the size of the loan receivable until it reaches the original sale price of $119,990. Eskimo then pays the full amount of the receivable, at which point Hammer records the following final entry:

	Debit	Credit
Cash	119,990	
Loan receivable		119,990

Also, note that the financing concept can be employed in reverse; that is, if a customer makes a deposit that the seller expects to retain for more than one year, the financing component of this arrangement should be recognized by the seller. Doing so properly reflects the economics of the arrangement, where the seller is using the cash of the customer to fund its purchase of materials and equipment for a project; if the seller had not provided the deposit, the seller would instead have needed to obtain financing.

There is assumed *not* to be a significant financing component to a contract in the presence of any of the following factors:

- *Advance payment.* The customer paid in advance, and the customer can specify when goods and services are to be delivered.
- *Variable component.* A large part of the consideration to be paid is variable, and payment timing will vary based on a future event that is not under the control of either party.
- *Non-financing reason.* The reason for the difference between the contractual consideration and the cash selling price exists for a reason other than financing, and the amount of the difference is proportional to the alternative reason.

EXAMPLE

Spinner Maintenance offers global technical support to the owners of rooftop solar power systems in exchange for a $400 fee. The fee pays for service that spans the first five years of the life of the power systems, and is purchased as part of the package of solar panels and initial installation work. This maintenance is intended to provide phone support to homeowners who are researching why their power systems are malfunctioning. The support does not include any replacement of solar panels for hail damage.

The support period is quite extensive, but Spinner concludes that there is no financing component to these sales, for the following reasons:

- The administrative cost of a monthly billing would be prohibitive, since the amount billed on a monthly basis would be paltry.
- Those more technologically proficient customers would be less likely to renew if they could pay on a more frequent basis, leaving Spinner with the highest-maintenance customers who require the most support.
- Customers are more likely to make use of the service if they are reminded of it by the arrival of monthly invoices.

In short, Spinner has several excellent reasons for structuring the payment plan to require an advance payment, all of which are centered on maintaining a reasonable level of profitability. The intent is not to provide financing to customers.

EXAMPLE

Glow Atomic sells a nuclear power plant to a French provincial government. The certification process for the plant is extensive, spanning a six-month test period. Accordingly, the local government builds into the contract a provision to withhold 20% of the contract price until completion of the test period. The rest of the payments are made on a milestone schedule, as the construction work progresses. Based on the circumstances and the amount of the withholding, the arrangement is considered to be non-financing, so Glow Atomic does not break out a financing component from the total consideration paid.

Noncash Consideration

If the customer will be paying with some form of noncash consideration, measure the consideration at its fair value as of the inception date of the contract. If it is not possible to measure the payment at its fair value, instead use the standalone selling price of the goods or services to be delivered to the customer. This approach also applies to payments made with equity instruments. In rare cases, the customer may supply the seller with goods or services that are intended to assist the seller in its fulfillment of the related contract. If the seller gains control of these assets or services, it should consider them to be noncash consideration paid by the customer.

EXAMPLE

Industrial Landscaping is hired by Pensive Corporation to mow the lawns and trim shrubbery at Pensive's corporate headquarters on a weekly basis throughout the year. Essentially the same service is provided each week. Pensive is a startup company with little excess cash, so it promises to pay Industrial with 25 shares of Pensive stock at the end of each week.

Industrial considers itself to have satisfied its performance obligation at the end of each week. Industrial should determine the transaction price as being the fair value of the shares at the end of each week, and recognizes this amount as revenue. There is no subsequent change in the amount of revenue recognized, irrespective of any changes in the fair value of the shares.

Payments to Customers

The contract may require the seller to pay consideration to the customer, perhaps in the form of credits or coupons that the customer can apply against the amounts it owes to the seller. This may also involve payments to third parties that have purchased the seller's goods or services from the original customer. If so, treat this consideration as a reduction of the transaction price. The following special situations may apply:

- *Customer supplies a good or service.* The customer may provide the seller with a distinct good or service; if so, the seller treats the payment as it would a payment to any supplier.
- *Supplier payment exceeds customer delivery.* If the customer provides a good or service to the seller, but the amount paid by the seller to the customer exceeds the fair value of the goods or services it receives in exchange, the excess of the payment is considered a reduction of the transaction price. If the fair value of the goods or services cannot be determined, then consider the entire amount paid by the seller to the customer to be a reduction of the transaction price.

If it is necessary to account for consideration paid to the customer as a reduction of the transaction price, do so when the later of the following two events have occurred:

- When the seller recognizes revenue related to its provision of goods or services to the customer; or
- When the seller either pays or promises to pay the consideration to the customer. The timing of this event could be derived from the customary business practices of the seller.

EXAMPLE

Dillinger Designs manufactures many types of hunting rifles. Dillinger enters into a one-year contract with Backwoods Survival, which has not previously engaged in rifle sales. Backwoods commits to purchase at least $240,000 of rifles from Dillinger during the contract period. Also, due to the hefty government-mandated safety requirements associated with the sale of rifles, Dillinger commits to pay $60,000 to Backwoods at the inception of the contract; these funds are intended to pay for a locking gun safe to be kept at each Backwoods store, as per firearms laws pertaining to retailers.

Dillinger determines that the $60,000 payment is to be treated as a reduction of the $240,000 sale price. Consequently, whenever Dillinger fulfills a performance obligation by shipping goods under the contract, it reduces the amount of revenue it would otherwise recognize by 25%, which reflects the proportion of the $60,000 payment related to locking gun safes of the $240,000 that Dillinger will be paid by Backwoods.

This topic is addressed again in the next chapter, in the Consideration Received from a Supplier section.

Refund Liabilities

In some situations, a seller may receive consideration from a customer, with the likelihood that the payment will be refunded. If so, the seller records a refund liability in the amount that the seller expects to refund back to the customer. The seller should review the amount of this liability at the end of each reporting period, to see if the amount should be altered.

Step Four: Allocate Prices to Obligations

Once the performance obligations and transaction prices associated with a contract have been identified, the next step is to allocate the transaction prices to the obligations. The basic rule is to allocate that price to a performance obligation that best reflects that amount of consideration to which the seller expects to be entitled when it satisfies each performance obligation. To determine this allocation, it is first necessary to estimate the standalone selling price of those distinct goods or services as of the inception date of the contract. If it is not possible to derive a standalone selling price, the seller must estimate it. This estimation should involve all relevant information that is reasonably available, such as:

- Competitive pressure on prices
- Costs incurred to manufacture or provide the item
- Item profit margins
- Pricing of other items in the same contract
- Standalone selling price of the item
- Supply and demand for the items in the market
- The seller's pricing strategy and practices
- The type of customer, distribution channel, or geographic region
- Third-party pricing

The following three approaches are acceptable ways in which to estimate a standalone selling price:

- *Adjusted market assessment.* This involves reviewing the market to estimate the price at which a customer in that market would be willing to pay for the goods and services in question. This can involve an examination of the prices of competitors for similar items and adjusting them to incorporate the seller's costs and margins.
- *Expected cost plus a margin.* This requires the seller to estimate the costs required to fulfill a performance obligation, and then add a margin to it to derive the estimated price.
- *Residual approach.* This involves subtracting all of the observable standalone selling prices from the total transaction price to arrive at the residual price remaining for allocation to any non-observable selling prices. This method can only be used if one of the following situations applies:
  - o The seller sells the good or service to other customers for a wide range of prices; or
  - o No price has yet been established for that item, and it has not yet been sold on a standalone basis.

The residual approach can be difficult to use when there are several goods or services with uncertain standalone selling prices. If so, it may be necessary to use a combination of methods to derive standalone selling prices, which should be used in the following order:

1. Estimate the aggregate amount of the standalone selling prices for all items having uncertain standalone selling prices, using the residual method.
2. Use another method to develop standalone selling prices for each item in this group, to allocate the aggregate amount of the standalone selling prices.

Once all standalone selling prices have been determined, allocate the transaction price amongst these distinct goods or services based on their relative standalone selling prices.

> **Tip:** Appropriate evidence of a standalone selling price is the observable price of a good or service when the seller sells it to a similar customer under similar circumstances.

Once the seller derives an approach for estimating a standalone selling price, it should consistently apply that method to the derivation of the standalone selling prices for other goods or services with similar characteristics.

EXAMPLE

Luminescence Corporation manufactures a wide range of light bulbs, and mostly sells into the wholesaler market. The company receives an order from the federal government for two million fluorescent bulbs, as well as for 100,000 units of a new bulb that operates outdoors at very low temperatures. Luminescence has not yet sold these new bulbs to anyone. The total price of the order is $7,000,000. Luminescence assigns $6,000,000 of the total price to the fluorescent bulbs, based on its own sales of comparable orders. This leaves $1,000,000 of the total price that is allocable to the low temperature bulbs. Since Luminescence has not yet established a price for these bulbs and has not sold them on a standalone basis, it is acceptable to allocate $1,000,000 to the low temperature bulbs under the residual approach.

If there is a subsequent change in the transaction price, allocate that change amongst the distinct goods or services based on the original allocation that was used at the inception of the contract. If this subsequent allocation is to a performance obligation that has already been completed and for which revenue has already been recognized, the result can be an increase or reduction in the amount of revenue recognized. This change in recognition should occur as soon as the subsequent change in the transaction price occurs.

Allocation of Price Discounts

It is assumed that a customer has received a discount on a bundled purchase of goods or services when the sum of the standalone prices for these items is greater than the consideration to be paid under the terms of a contract. The discount can be allocated to a specific item within the bundled purchase, if there is observable evidence that the discount was intended for that item. In order to do so, all of the following criteria must apply:

1. Each distinct item in the bundle is regularly sold on a standalone basis;
2. A bundle of some of these distinct items is regularly sold at a discount to their standalone selling prices; and

3. The discount noted in the second point is essentially the same as the discount in the contract, and there is observable evidence linking the entire contract discount to that bundle of distinct items.

If this allocation system is used, the seller must employ it before using the residual approach noted earlier in this section. Doing so ensures that the discount is not applied to the other performance obligations in the contract to which prices have not yet been allocated.

In all other cases, the discount is to be allocated amongst all of the items in the bundle. In this latter situation, the allocation is to be made based on the standalone selling prices of all of the performance obligations in the contract.

EXAMPLE

The Hegemony Toy Company sells board games that re-enact famous battles. Hegemony regularly sells the following three board games:

Product	Standalone Selling Price
Hastings Battle Game	$120
Stalingrad Battle Game	100
Waterloo Battle Game	80
Total	$300

Hegemony routinely sells the Stalingrad and Waterloo products as a bundle for $120.

Hegemony enters into a contract with the War Games International website to sell War Games the set of three games for $240, which is a 20% discount from the standard price. Deliveries of these games to War Games will be at different times, so the related performance obligations will be settled on different dates.

The $60 discount would normally be apportioned among all three products based on their standalone selling prices. However, because Hegemony routinely sells the Stalingrad/Waterloo bundle for a $60 discount, it is evident that the entire discount should be allocated to these two products.

If Hegemony later delivers the Stalingrad and Waterloo games to War Games on different dates, it should allocate the $60 discount between the two products based on their standalone selling prices. Thus, $33.33 should be allocated to the Stalingrad game and $26.67 to the Waterloo game. The allocation calculation is:

Game	Allocation
Stalingrad	($100 individual game price ÷ $180 combined price) × $60 discount = $33.33
Waterloo	($80 individual game price ÷ $180 combined price) × $60 discount = $26.67

If the two games are instead delivered at the same time, there is no need to conduct the preceding allocation. Instead, the discount can be assigned to them both as part of a single performance obligation.

Allocation of Variable Consideration

There may be a variable amount of consideration associated with a contract. This consideration may apply to the contract as a whole, or to just a portion of it. For example, a bonus payment may be tied to the completion of a specific performance obligation. It is allowable to allocate variable consideration to a specific performance obligation or a distinct good or service within a contract when the variable payment terms are specifically tied to the seller's efforts to satisfy the performance obligation.

EXAMPLE

Nova Corporation contracts with the Deep Field Scanning Authority to construct two three-meter telescopes that will operate in tandem in the low-humidity Atacama Desert in Chile. The terms of the contract include a provision that can increase the allowable price charged, if the commodity cost of the titanium required to build the telescope frames increases. Based on the prices stated in forward contracts at the contract inception date, it is likely that this variable cost element will increase the transaction price by $250,000. The variable component of the price is allocated to each of the telescopes equally.

Subsequent Price Changes

There are a number of reasons why the transaction price could change after a contract has begun, such as the resolution of uncertain events that were in need of clarification at the contract inception date. When there is a price change, the amount of the change is to be allocated to the performance obligations on the same basis used for the original price allocation at the inception of the contract. This has the following ramifications:

- Do not re-allocate prices based on subsequent changes in the standalone selling prices of goods or services.
- When there is a price change and that price is allocated, the result may be the recognition of additional or reduced revenue that is to be recognized in the period when the transaction price changes.
- When there has been a contract modification prior to a price change, the price allocation is conducted in two steps. First, allocate the price change to those performance obligations identified prior to the modification if the price change is associated with variable consideration promised before modification. In all other cases, allocate the price change to those performance obligations still remaining to be settled as of the modification date.

The result should be a reported level of cumulative revenue that matches the amount of revenue an organization would have recognized if it had the most recent information at the inception date of the contract.

Step Five: Recognize Revenue

Revenue is to be recognized as goods or services are transferred to the customer. This transference is considered to occur when the customer gains control over the good or service. Indicators of this date include the following:

- When the seller has the right to receive payment.
- When the customer has legal title to the transferred asset. This can still be the case even when the seller retains title to protect it against the customer's failure to pay.
- When physical possession of the asset has been transferred by the seller. Possession can be inferred even when goods are held elsewhere on consignment, or by the seller under a bill-and-hold arrangement. Under a bill-and-hold arrangement, the seller retains goods on behalf of the customer, but still recognizes revenue. This topic is addressed in the Bill-and-Hold Arrangements section in the next chapter.
- When the customer has taken on the significant risks and rewards of ownership related to the asset transferred by the seller. For example, the customer can now sell, pledge, or exchange the asset.
- When the customer accepts the asset.
- When the customer can prevent other entities from using or obtaining benefits from the asset.

It is possible that a performance obligation will be transferred over time, rather than as of a specific point in time. If so, revenue recognition occurs when any one of the following criteria are met:

- *Immediate use.* The customer both receives and consumes the benefit provided by the seller as performance occurs. This situation arises if another entity would not need to re-perform work completed to date if the other entity were to take over the remaining performance obligation. Routine and recurring services typically fall into this classification.

EXAMPLE

Long-Haul Freight contracts to deliver a load of goods from Los Angeles to Boston. This service should be considered a performance obligation that is transferred over time, despite the fact that the customer only benefits from the goods once they are delivered. The reason for the designation as a transference over time is that, if a different trucking firm were to take over partway through the journey, the replacement firm would not have to re-perform the freight hauling that has already been completed to date.

EXAMPLE

Maid Marian is a nationwide home cleaning service run by friars within the Franciscan Order. Its customers both receive and simultaneously consume the cleaning services provided by its staff. Consequently, the services provided by Maid Marian are considered to be performance obligations satisfied over time.

- *Immediate enhancement*. The seller creates or enhances an asset controlled by the customer as performance occurs. This asset can be tangible or intangible.
- *No alternative use*. The seller's performance does not create an asset for which there is an alternative use to the seller (such as selling it to a different customer). In addition, the contract gives the seller an enforceable right to payment for the performance that has been completed to date. A lack of alternative use happens when a contract restricts the seller from directing the asset to another use, or when there are practical limitations on doing so, such as the incurrence of significant economic losses to direct the asset elsewhere. The determination of whether an asset has an alternative use is made at the inception of the contract, and cannot be subsequently altered unless both parties to the contract approve a modification that results in a substantive change in the performance obligation.

Construction contracts are likely to be designated as being performance obligations that are transferred over time. Under this approach, they can use the percentage-of-completion method to recognize revenue, rather than the completed contract method. This means that they can recognize revenue as a construction project progresses, rather than waiting until the end of the project to recognize any revenue.

EXAMPLE

Oberlin Acoustics is contractually obligated to deliver a highly-customized version of its Rhino brand electric guitar to a diva-grade European rock star. The contract clearly states that this customized version can only be delivered to the designated customer, and it is likely that this individual would pursue legal action if Oberlin were to attempt to sell it elsewhere (such as to the lead guitarist of a rival band). Also, Oberlin might have to incur significant costs to reconfigure the guitar for sale to a different customer. In this situation, there is no alternative use.

However, if Oberlin had instead contracted to deliver one of its standard Rhino brand guitars, the company could easily transfer the asset to a different customer, since the products are essentially interchangeable. In this case, there would be a clear alternative use.

EXAMPLE

Tesla Power Company is hired by a local government to construct one of its new, compact fusion power plants in the remote hinterlands of Malawi. There is clearly no alternative use for the power plant, since Tesla would have to incur major costs to dismantle the facility and truck it out of the remote area before it could be sold to a different customer. However, the contract states that 50% of the price will be paid at the end of the contract period, and there is no enforceable right to any payment; this means that Tesla must consider its performance obligation to be satisfied as of a point in time, rather than over time.

EXAMPLE

Hassle Corporation is in talks with a potential acquirer. The acquirer insists that Hassle have soil tests conducted in the area around its main production facility, to see if there has been any leakage of pollutants. Hassle engages Wilson Environmental to conduct these tests, which is a three-month process. The contract includes a clause that Wilson will be paid for its costs plus a 20% profit if Hassle cancels the contract. The acquisition talks break off after two months, so Hassle notifies Wilson that it no longer needs the environmental report. Since Wilson cannot possibly sell the information it has collected to a different customer, there is no alternative use. Also, since Wilson has an enforceable right to payment for all work completed to date, the company can recognize revenue over time by measuring its progress toward satisfying the performance obligation.

Measurement of Progress Completion

When a performance obligation is being completed over a period of time, the seller recognizes revenue through the application of a progress completion method. The goal of this method is to determine the progress of the seller in achieving complete satisfaction of its performance obligation. This method is to be consistently applied over time, and shall be re-measured at the end of each reporting period.

> **Note:** The method used to measure progress should be applied consistently for a particular performance obligation, as well as across multiple contracts that have obligations with similar characteristics. Otherwise, reported revenue will not be comparable across different reporting periods.

Both output methods and input methods are considered acceptable for determining progress completion. The method chosen should incorporate due consideration of the nature of the goods or services being provided to the customer. The following subsections address the use of output and input methods.

Output Methods

An output method recognizes revenue based on a comparison of the value to the customer of goods and services transferred to date to the remaining goods and services not yet transferred. There are numerous ways to measure output, including:

- Surveys of performance to date
- Milestones reached
- The passage of time
- The number of units delivered
- The number of units produced

Another output method that may be acceptable is the amount of consideration that the seller has the right to invoice, such as billable hours. This approach works when the seller has a right to invoice an amount that matches the amount of performance completed to date.

The number of units delivered or produced may not be an appropriate output method in situations where there is a large amount of work-in-process, since the value associated with unfinished goods may be so substantial that revenue could be materially under-reported.

The method picked should closely adhere to the concept of matching the seller's progress toward satisfying the performance obligation. It is not always possible to use an output method, since the cost of collecting the necessary information can be prohibitive, or progress may not be directly observable.

EXAMPLE

Viking Fitness operates a regional chain of fitness clubs that are oriented toward younger, very athletic people (which may explain why each store is located next to a vitamin supplements shop). Members pay a $1,200 annual fee, which gives them access to all of the clubs in the chain during all operating hours. In effect, Viking's performance obligation is to keep its facilities open for use by members, irrespective of whether they actually use the facilities. Clearly, this situation calls for measurement of progress completion based on the passage of time. Accordingly, Viking recognizes revenue from its annual customer payments at the rate of $100 per member per month.

Input Methods

An input method derives the amount of revenue to be recognized based on the to-date effort required by the seller to satisfy a performance obligation relative to the total estimated amount of effort required. Examples of possible inputs are costs incurred, labor hours expended, and machine hours used. If there are situations where the effort expended does not directly relate to the transfer of goods or services to a customer, do not use that input. The following are situations where the input used could lead to incorrect revenue recognition:

- The costs incurred are higher than expected, due to seller inefficiencies. For example, the seller may have wasted a higher-than-expected amount of raw materials in the performance of its obligations under a contract.
- The costs incurred are not in proportion to the progress of the seller toward satisfying the performance obligation. For example, the seller might purchase a large amount of materials at the inception of a contract, which comprise a significant part of the total price.

Tip: If the effort expended to satisfy performance obligations occur evenly through the performance period, consider recognizing revenue on the straight-line basis through the performance period.

EXAMPLE

Eskimo Construction is hired to build a weather observatory in Barrow, Alaska, which is estimated to be a six-month project. Utilities are a major concern, especially since the facility is too far away from town for a power line to be run out to it. Accordingly, a large part of the construction cost is a diesel-powered turbine generator. The total cost that Eskimo intends to incur for the project is:

Turbine cost	$1,250,000
All other costs	2,750,000
Total costs	$4,000,000

The turbine is to be delivered and paid for at the beginning of the construction project, but will not be incorporated into the facility until late summer, when the building is scheduled to be nearly complete.

Eskimo intends to use an input method to derive the amount of revenue, using costs incurred. However, this approach runs afoul of the turbine cost, since the immediate expenditure for the turbine gives the appearance of the project being 31.25% complete before work has even begun. Accordingly, Eskimo excludes the cost of the turbine from its input method calculations, only using the other costs as the basis for deriving revenue.

The situation described in the preceding example is quite common, since materials are typically procured at the inception of a contract, rather than being purchased in equal quantities over the duration of the contract. Consequently, the accountant should be particularly mindful of this issue and incorporate it into any revenue recognition calculations based on an input method.

A method based on output is preferred, since it most faithfully depicts the performance of the seller under the terms of a contract. However, an input-based method is certainly allowable if using it would be less costly for the seller, while still providing a reasonable proxy for the ongoing measurement of progress.

Change in Estimate

Whichever method is used, be sure to update it over time to reflect changes in the seller's performance to date. If there is a change in the measurement of progress, treat the change as a change in accounting estimate.

A change in accounting estimate occurs when there is an adjustment to the carrying amount of an asset or liability, or the subsequent accounting for it. Changes in accounting estimate occur relatively frequently, and so would require a considerable effort to make an ongoing series of retroactive changes to prior financial statements. Instead, GAAP only requires that changes in accounting estimate be accounted for in the period of change and thereafter. Thus, no retrospective change is required or allowed.

Progress Measurement

It is only possible to recognize the revenue associated with progress completion if it is possible for the seller to measure the seller's progress. If the seller lacks reliable progress information, it will not be possible to recognize the revenue associated with a contract over time. There may be cases where the measurement of progress completion is more difficult during the early stages of a contract. If so, it is allowable for the seller to instead recognize just enough revenue to recover its costs in satisfying its performance obligations, thereby deferring the recognition of other revenue until such time as the measurement system yields more accurate results.

Right of Return

A common right granted to customers is to allow them to return goods to the seller within a certain period of time following the customer's receipt of the goods. This return may take the form of a refund of any amounts paid, a general credit that can be applied against other billings from the seller, or an exchange for a different unit. The proper accounting for this right of return involves three components, which are:

1. Recognize the net amount of revenue to which the seller expects to be entitled after all product returns have been factored into the sale.
2. A refund liability that encompasses the number of units that the seller expects to have returned to it.
3. An asset based on the right to recover products from customers who have demanded refunds. This asset represents a reduction in the cost of goods sold. The amount is initially based on the former carrying amount of the inventory, less recovery costs and expected reductions in the value of the returned products.

This accounting requires the seller to update its assessment of future product returns at the end of each reporting period, both for the refund liability and the recovery asset. This update may result in a change in the amount of revenue recognized.

Note: When a customer exchanges one product for another product with the same characteristics (such as an exchange of one size shirt for another), this is not considered a return.

EXAMPLE

Ninja Cutlery sells high-end ceramic knife sets through its on-line store and through select retailers. All customers pay up-front in cash. In the most recent month, Ninja sold 5,000 knife sets, which sold for an average price of $250 each ($1,250,000 in total). The unit cost is $150. Based on the history of actual returns over the preceding 12-month period, Ninja can expect that 200 of the sets (4% of the total) will be returned under the company's returns policy. Recovery costs are immaterial, and Ninja expects to be able to repackage and sell all returned products for a profit. Based on this information, Ninja records the following transactions when the knife sets are originally delivered:

	Debit	Credit
Cash	1,250,000	
Revenue		1,200,000
Refund liability		50,000

	Debit	Credit
Cost of goods sold	720,000	
Recovery asset	30,000	
Inventory		750,000

In these entries, the refund liability is calculated as the 200 units expected to be returned, multiplied by the average price of $250 each. The recovery asset is calculated as the 200 units expected to be returned, multiplied by the unit cost of $150.

Consistency

The preceding five steps must be applied consistently to all customer contracts that have similar characteristics, and under similar circumstances. The intent is to create a system of revenue recognition that can be relied upon to yield consistent results.

Contract Modifications

A contract modification occurs when there is a scope or price change to the contract, and the change is approved by both signatories to the contract. Other terms may be used for a contract modification, such as a change order. It is possible that a contract modification exists, despite the presence of a dispute between the parties concerning scope or price. All of the relevant facts and circumstances must be considered when determining whether there is an enforceable contract modification that can impact revenue recognition.

If a change in contract scope has already been approved, but the corresponding change in price to reflect the scope change is still under discussion, the seller must estimate the change in price. This estimate is based on the criteria used to determine variable consideration. See the Variable Consideration sub-section for more information.

Treatment as Separate Contract

There are circumstances under which a contract modification might be accounted for as a separate contract. For this to be the case, the following two conditions must both be present:

- *Distinct change.* The scope has increased, to encompass new goods or services that are distinct from those offered in the original contract.
- *Price change.* The price has increased enough to encompass the standalone prices of the additional goods and services, adjusted for the circumstances related to that specific contract.

When these circumstances are met, there is an economic difference between a modified contract for the additional goods or services and a situation where an entirely new contract has been created.

EXAMPLE

Blitz Communications is buying one million cell phone batteries from Creekside Industrial. The parties decide to alter the contract to add the purchase of 200,000 battery chargers for a price increase of $2.8 million. The associated price increase includes a 30% discount, which Creekside was already offering to Blitz under the terms of the original contract. This contract change reflects a distinct change that adds new goods to the contract, and includes an associated price change that has been adjusted for the discount terms of the contract. This contract modification can be accounted for as a separate contract.

Treatment as Continuing Contract

It may not be possible to treat a contract modification as a separate contract. If so, there are likely to be goods or services not yet transferred to the customer as of the modification date. The seller can account for these residual deliveries using one of the following methods:

- *Remainder is distinct.* If the remaining goods or services to be delivered are distinct from those already delivered under the contract, account for the modification as a cancellation of the old contract and creation of a new one. In this case, the consideration that should be allocated to the remaining performance obligations is the sum total of:
  - The original consideration promised by the customer but not yet received; and
  - The new consideration associated with the modification.

EXAMPLE

Grizzly Golf Carts, maker of sturdy golf carts for overweight golfers, contracts with a local suburban golf course to deliver two golf carts for a total price of $12,000. The carts are different models, but have the same standalone price, so Grizzly allocates $6,000 of the transaction price to each cart. One cart is delivered immediately, so Grizzly recognizes $6,000 of revenue. Before the second cart can be delivered, the golf course customer requests that a third cart be added to the contract; this is a heftier cart that has a built-in barbecue grill. The contract price is increased by $8,000, which is less than the $10,000 standalone price of this model.

Since the second and third carts are distinct from the first cart model, there is a distinct change in the contract, which necessitates treating the change as a new contract. Accordingly, the second and third carts are treated as though they are part of a new contract, with the remaining $14,000 of the transaction price totally allocated to the new contract.

EXAMPLE

As noted in an earlier example, Nova Corporation contracted with the Deep Field Scanning Authority to construct two three-meter telescopes. The terms of the contract included a provision that could increase the allowable price charged by $250,000, with this price being apportioned equally between the two telescopes. One month into the contract period, Deep Field completely alters the configuration of the second telescope, from a reflector to a catadioptric model. The change is so significant that this telescope can now be considered a separate contract. However, since the variable price was already apportioned at the inception of the original contract, the $125,000 allocated to each telescope will continue. This is because the variable consideration was promised prior to the contract modification.

- *Remainder is not distinct.* If the remaining goods or services to be delivered are not distinct from those already delivered under the contract, account for the modification as part of the existing contract. This results in an adjustment to the recognized amount of revenue (up or down) as of the modification date. Thus, the adjustment involves calculating a change in the amount of revenue recognized on a cumulative catch-up basis.

EXAMPLE

Domicilio Corporation enters into a contract to construct the world headquarters building of the International Mushroom Farmers' Cooperative. Mushroom requires its architects to be true to the name of the organization, with the result being a design for a squat, dark building with no windows, high humidity, and a unique waste recycling system. Domicilio has not encountered such a design before, and so incorporates a cautious stance into its assumptions regarding the contract terms.

The contract terms state that Domicilio will be paid a total of $12,000,000, broken into a number of milestone payments. There is also a $100,000 on-time completion bonus. At the inception of the contract, Domicilio expects the following financial results:

Transaction price	$12,000,000
Expected costs	9,000,000
Expected profit (25%)	$3,000,000

The project manager anticipates trouble with several parts of the construction project, and advises strongly against including any part of the completion bonus in the transaction price.

At the end of seven months, the project manager is surprised to find that Domicilio is on target to complete the work on time. Also, the company has completed 65% of its performance obligation, based on the $5,850,000 of costs incurred to date relative to the total amount of expected costs. Through this point, the company has recognized the following revenues and costs:

Revenue	$7,800,000
Costs	5,850,000
Gross profit	$1,950,000

The project manager is still uncomfortable with recognizing any part of the completion bonus.

With one month to go on the project, the project manager finally allows that Domicilio will likely complete the project one week early, though he has completely lost all interest in eating mushrooms. At this point, the company has completed 92.5% of its performance obligation (based on costs incurred), so the controller recognizes an additional $92,500 for that portion of the $100,000 on-time completion bonus that has already been earned.

- *Mix of elements*. If the remaining goods or services to be delivered are comprised of a mix of distinct and not-distinct elements, separately identify the different elements and account for them as per the dictates of the preceding two methods.

Entitlement to Payment

At all points over the duration of a contract, the seller should have the right to payment for the performance completed to date, if the customer were to cancel the contract for reasons other than the seller's failure to perform. The amount of this payment should approximate the selling price of the goods or services transferred to the customer to date; this means that costs are recovered, plus a reasonable profit margin. This reasonable profit margin should be one of the following:

- A reasonable proportion of the expected profit margin, based on the extent of the total performance completed prior to contract termination; or

- A reasonable return on the cost of capital that the seller has experienced on its cost of capital for similar contracts, if the margin on this particular contract is higher than the return the seller typically generates from this type of contract.

An entitlement to payment depends on contractual factors, such as only being paid when certain milestones are reached or when the customer is completely satisfied with a deliverable. There may not be an entitlement to payment if one of these contractual factors is present. Further, there may be legal precedents or legislation that may interfere with or bolster an entitlement to payment. For example:

- There may be a legal precedent that gives the seller the right to payment for all performance to date, even though this right is not clarified within the contract terms.
- Legal precedent may reveal that other sellers having similar rights to payment in their contracts have not succeeded in obtaining payment.
- The seller may not have attempted to enforce its right to payment in the past, which may have rendered its rights legally unenforceable.

Conversely, the terms of a contract may not legally allow a customer to terminate a contract. If so, and the customer still attempts to terminate the contract, the seller may be entitled to continue to provide goods or services to the customer, and require the customer to pay the amounts stated in the contract. In this type of situation, the seller has an enforceable right to payment.

An enforceable right to payment may not match the payment schedule stated in a contract. The payment schedule does not necessarily sync with the seller's right to payment for performance. For example, the customer could have insisted upon delayed payment dates in the payment schedule in order to more closely match its ability to make payments to the seller.

EXAMPLE

A customer of Hodgson Industrial Design pays a $50,000 nonrefundable upfront payment to Hodgson at the inception of a contract to overhaul the design of the customer's main product. The customer does not like Hodgson's initial set of design prototypes, and cancels the contract. On the cancellation date, Hodgson's billable hours on the project sum to $65,000. Hodgson has an enforceable right to retain the $50,000 it has already been paid. The right to be paid for the remaining $15,000 depends on the contract terms and legal precedents.

Contract-Related Costs

Thus far, the discussion has centered on the recognition of revenue – but what about the costs that an organization incurs to fulfill a contract? In this section, we separately address the accounting for the costs incurred to initially obtain a contract, costs incurred during a contract, and how these costs are to be charged to expense.

Costs to Obtain a Contract

An organization may incur certain costs to obtain a contract. If so, it is allowable to record these costs as an asset, and amortize them over the life of the contract. The following conditions apply:

- The costs must be incremental; that is, they would not have been incurred if the organization had not obtained the contract.
- If the amortization period will be one year or some lesser period, it is allowable to simply charge these costs to expense as incurred.
- There is an expectation that the costs will be recovered.

An example of a contract-related cost that could be recorded as an asset and amortized is the sales commission associated with a sale, though as a practical expedient it is usually charged to expense as incurred.

EXAMPLE

A water engineering firm bids on a contract to investigate the level of silt accumulation in the Oswego Canal in New York, and wins the bid. The firm incurs the following costs as part of its bidding process.

Staff time to prepare proposal	$18,000
Printing fees	2,500
Travel costs	5,000
Commissions paid to sales staff	15,000
	$40,500

The firm must charge the staff time, printing fees, and travel costs to expense as incurred, since it would have incurred these expenses even if the bid had failed. Only the commissions paid to the sales staff can be considered a contract asset, since that cost should be recovered through its future billings for consulting services.

Costs to Fulfill a Contract

In general, any costs required to fulfill a contract should be recognized as assets, as long as they meet all of these criteria:

- The costs are tied to a specific contract;
- The costs will be used to satisfy future performance obligations; and
- There is an expectation that the costs will be recovered.

Costs that are considered to relate directly to a contract include the following:

- *Direct labor.* Includes the wages of those employees directly engaged in providing services to the customer.
- *Direct materials.* Includes the supplies consumed in the provision of services to the customer.
- *Cost allocations.* Includes those costs that relate directly to the contract, such as the cost of managing the contract, project supervision, and depreciation of the equipment used to fulfill the contract.
- *Chargeable costs.* Includes those costs that the contract explicitly states can be charged to the customer.
- *Other costs.* Includes costs that would only be incurred because the seller entered into the contract, such as payments to subcontractors providing services to the customer.

Other costs are to be charged to expense as incurred, rather than being classified as contract assets. These costs include:

- *Administration.* General and administrative costs, unless the contract terms explicitly state that they can be charged to the contract.
- *Indistinguishable.* Costs for which it is not possible to determine whether they relate to unsatisfied or satisfied performance obligations. In this case, the default assumption is that they relate to satisfied performance obligations.
- *Past performance costs.* Any costs incurred that relate to performance obligations that have already been fulfilled.
- *Waste.* The costs of resources wasted in the contract fulfillment process, which were not included in the contract price.

EXAMPLE

Tele-Service International enters into a contract to take over the phone customer service function of Artisan's Delight, a manufacturer of hand-woven wool shopping bags. Tele-Service incurs a cost of $50,000 to construct an interface between the inventory and customer service systems of Artisan's Delight and its own call database. This cost relates to activities needed to fulfill the requirements of the contract, but does not result in the provision of any services to Artisan's Delight. This cost should be amortized over the term of the contract.

Tele-Service assigns four of its employees on a full-time basis to handle incoming customer calls from Artisan's customers. Though this group is providing services to the customer, it is not generating or enhancing the resources of Tele-Service, and so its cost cannot be recognized as an asset. Instead, the cost of these employees is charged to expense as incurred.

Amortization of Costs

When contract-related costs have been recognized as assets, they should be amortized on a systematic basis that reflects the timing of the transfer of related goods and services to the customer. If there is a change in the anticipated timing of the transfer of goods and services to the customer, update the amortization to reflect this change. This is considered a change in accounting estimate.

Impairment of Costs

The seller should recognize an impairment loss in the current period when the carrying amount of an asset associated with a contract is greater than the remaining payments to be received from the customer. The calculation is:

Remaining consideration to be received[1] – Costs not yet recognized as expenses

= Impairment amount (if result is a negative figure)

> **Note:** When calculating possible impairment, adjust the amount of the remaining consideration to be received for the effects of the customer's credit risk.

It is not allowable to reverse an impairment loss on contract assets that has already been recognized.

Exclusions

The revenue recognition rules contained within Topic 606 do not apply to the following areas, for which more specific recognition standards apply:

- Lease contracts
- Financial services contracts
- Financial instruments involving receivables, investments, liabilities, debt, derivatives, hedging, or transfers and servicing
- Guarantees, not including product or service warranties
- Nonmonetary exchanges between entities in the same line of business, where the intent is to facilitate sales transactions to existing or potential customers

---

EXAMPLE

Two distributors of heating oil swap stocks of different grades of heating oil, so that they can better meet the forecasted demand of their customers. No revenue recognition occurs in this situation, since the two parties are in the same line of business and the intent of the transaction is to facilitate sales to potential customers.

Since Topic 606 only applies to contracts with customers, there are a number of transactions that do not incorporate these elements, and so are not covered by the provisions

---

[1] The remaining consideration to be received includes the residual amount expected to be received in the future and the amount already received but which has not yet been recognized as revenue.

of this Topic. Consequently, the following transactions and events are not covered:

- Dividends received
- Non-exchange transactions, such as donations received
- Changes in regulatory assets and liabilities caused by alternative revenue programs for rate-regulated entities

Applicability

The revenue recognition principles stated in Topic 606 are applicable to all entities, including nonprofit entities (though the accounting for donations is unchanged, and is described in the next chapter).

Topic 606 is to be applied retrospectively to any comparative financial statements appearing alongside the current financial statements, using one of the following two methods:

- *To each prior period presented.* It is not necessary to restate any contracts that begin and end within the same annual reporting period. If there was variable consideration in a completed contract, it is acceptable to use the transaction price on the contract completion date. It is not necessary to disclose that portion of the transaction price allocated to any remaining performance obligations, nor is it necessary to explain when the entity expects to recognize the residual income. This approach greatly reduces the burden of retrospective application in an organization that deals with large numbers of short-term contracts.
- *With cumulative effect noted.* Include the cumulative effect of the initial application of Topic 606 as of the initial application date. Under this method of application, disclose the monetary effect on each financial statement line item as compared to results before application. Also note the reasons for any significant variances between these two amounts. This means that comparative years listed in the financial statements would not be restated for contracts not completed as of the initial application date.

Summary

A key benefit of Topic 606 is that the recognition of revenue from contracts with customers will now be quite consistent across a number of contract types and industries. Previously, industry-specific standards did not always treat essentially the same types of transactions in a similar manner. This may mean that some industries, such as software, may experience significant recognition changes, since they were previously governed by highly specific recognition rules. Some entities, irrespective of their industry, may find that their recognition accounting will also change to a considerable extent if they had previously been using an interpretation of the existing standards that is no longer valid. For many industries, however, especially those involving retail transactions, the net effect of this new standard is minimal.

An interesting issue related to revenue recognition is that Topic 606 is almost entirely principles-based, where the general conceptual aspects of revenue recognition are outlined, rather than imposing massive amounts of rules-based specificity. This principles-based approach is the hallmark of international financial reporting standards, which have been largely constructed on this basis. The approach is quite unusual for GAAP, which is largely rules-based. It will be interesting to see if the principles-based approach will now be applied to additional accounting standards issued for GAAP.

Chapter 2
Other Revenue Topics

Introduction

In Chapter 1, we addressed the main concepts of revenue recognition as they apply to contracts with customers. However, this still leaves a number of peripheral topics that are closely related *to* revenue recognition, or which are essentially special cases *of* revenue recognition. We address these peripheral topics in the following sections, listing them in alphabetical order. The topics range from relatively rare ones, such as bill-and-hold arrangements, to common events, such as consignments, the sale of assets, and licensing arrangements.

Bill-and-Hold Arrangements

There is a bill-and-hold arrangement between a seller and customer when the seller bills the customer, but initially retains physical possession of the goods that were sold; the goods are transferred to the customer at a later date. This situation may arise if a customer does not initially have the storage space available for the goods it has ordered.

In a bill-and-hold arrangement, the seller must determine when the customer gains control of the goods, since this point in time indicates when the seller can recognize revenue. Customer control can be difficult to discern when the goods are still located on the premises of the seller. The following are indicators of customer control:

- The customer can direct the use of the goods, no matter where they are located
- The customer can obtain substantially all of the remaining benefits of the goods

Further, the following conditions must all be present for the seller to recognize revenue under a bill-and-hold arrangement:

- *Adequate reason.* There must be a substantive reason why the seller is continuing to store the goods, such as at the direct request of the customer.
- *Alternate use.* The seller must not be able to redirect the goods, either to other customers or for internal use.
- *Complete.* The product must be complete in all respects and ready for transfer to the customer.
- *Identification.* The goods must have been identified specifically as belonging to the customer.

Under a bill-and-hold arrangement, the seller may have a performance obligation to act as the custodian for the goods being held at its facility. If so, the seller may need to allocate a portion of the transaction price to the custodial function, and recognize this revenue over the course of the custodial period.

EXAMPLE

Micron Metallic operates stamping machines that produce parts for washing machines. Micron's general manager has recently decided to implement the just-in-time philosophy throughout the company, which includes sourcing goods with suppliers who are located as close to Micron as possible. One of these suppliers is Horton Corporation, which designs and builds stamping machines for Micron. In a recent contract, Micron buys a customized stamping machine and a set of spare parts intended for that machine. Since Micron is implementing just-in-time concepts, it does not want to store the spare parts on its premises, and instead asks Horton to store the parts in its facility, which is just down the street from the Micron factory.

Micron's receiving staff travels to the Horton facility to inspect the parts and formally accepts them. Horton also sets them aside in a separate storage area, and flags them as belonging to Micron. Since the parts are customized, they cannot be used to fulfill any other customer orders. Under the just-in-time system, Horton commits to having the parts ready for delivery to Micron within ten minutes of receiving a shipping order.

The arrangement can clearly be defined as a bill-and-hold situation. Consequently, Horton should apportion the transaction price between the stamping machine, the spare parts, and the custodial service involved in storing the parts on behalf of Micron. The revenue associated with the machine and parts can be recognized at once, while the revenue associated with the custodial service can be recognized with the passage of time.

Consideration Received from a Supplier

A supplier may pay consideration to its customer, which may be in the form of cash, credits, coupons, and so forth. The customer can then apply this consideration to payments that it owes to the supplier, thereby reducing its net accounts payable.

The proper accounting for this type of consideration is to reduce the purchase price of the goods or services that the customer is acquiring from the supplier in the amount of the consideration received. If the consideration received relates to the customer attaining a certain amount of purchasing volume with the supplier (i.e., a volume discount), recognize the consideration as a reduction of the purchase price of the underlying transactions. This recognition can be made if attainment of the consideration is both probable and can be reasonably estimated. If these criteria cannot be met, then wait for the triggering milestones, and recognize them as the milestones are reached. Factors that can make it more difficult to determine whether this type of consideration is probable or reasonably estimated include:

- *Duration.* The relationship between the consideration to be received and purchase amounts spans a long period of time.
- *Experience.* The customer has no historical experience with similar products, or cannot apply its experience to changing circumstances.

- *External factors.* External factors can influence the underlying activity, such as changes in demand.
- *Prior adjustments.* It has been necessary to make significant adjustments to similar types of expected consideration in the past.

EXAMPLE

Puller Corporation manufactures plastic door knobs. Its primary raw material is polymer resin, which it purchases in pellet form from a regional chemical facility. Puller will receive a 2% volume discount if it purchases at least $500,000 of pellets from the supplier by the end of the calendar year. Puller has a long-term relationship with this supplier, has routinely earned the discount for the last five years, and plans to place orders in this year that will comfortably exceed the $500,000 mark. Accordingly, Puller accrues the 2% discount as a reduction of the purchase price of its pellet purchases throughout the year.

EXAMPLE

Puller has just entered into a new relationship with another supplier that will deliver black dye to the factory for inclusion in all of the company's black door knob products. This supplier offers a 5% discount if purchases exceed $50,000 for the calendar year. Puller has not sold this color of door knob before and so has no idea of what customer demand may be. Given the high level of uncertainty regarding the probability of being awarded the discount, Puller elects to record all purchases at their full price, and will re-evaluate the probability of attaining the discount as the year progresses.

The only exceptions to this accounting are:

- When the customer specifically transfers an asset to the supplier in exchange. If so, the customer treats the transaction as it would any sale to one of its customers in the normal course of business. If the amount paid by the supplier is higher than the standalone selling price of the item transferred to the supplier, the customer should account for the excess amount as a reduction of the purchase price of any goods or services received from the supplier.
- The supplier is reimbursing the customer for selling costs that the customer incurred to sell the supplier's products to third parties. If so, the amount of cash received is used to reduce the indicated selling costs. If the amount paid by the supplier is greater than the amount for which the customer applied for reimbursement, record the excess as a reduction of the cost of sales.
- The consideration is related to sales incentives offered by manufacturers who are selling through a reseller. When the reseller is receiving compensation in exchange for honoring incentives related to the manufacturer's products, the reseller records the amount received as a reduction of its cost of sales. This situation only arises when all of the following conditions apply:
  - o The customer can tender the incentive to any reseller as part of its payment for the product;

o The reseller receives reimbursement from the manufacturer based on the face amount of the incentive;
o The reimbursement terms to the reseller are only determined from the incentive terms offered to consumers; they are not negotiated between the manufacturer and reseller; and
o The reseller is an agent of the manufacturer in regard to the sales incentive transaction.

If only a few or none of these criteria are met for a sales incentive offered by a manufacturer, account for the transaction as a reduction of the purchase price of the goods or services that the reseller acquired from the manufacturer. If all of the criteria *are* met, consider the transaction to be a revenue-generating activity for the reseller.

Consignment Arrangements

There may be a situation in which a seller delivers goods to another party, which are to then be sold to end customers. The intermediate party in this arrangement is typically a distributor or retailer. If the intermediate party has gained control of the goods upon receipt, the seller can recognize revenue related to the delivery. However, if the intermediate party has not gained control, this is considered to be a consignment arrangement. Under a consignment arrangement, the seller cannot recognize any revenue until the goods are eventually sold to end customers. Possible indicators that a consignment arrangement is present include the following:

- The goods are controlled by the seller until a later event, such as their sale to an end customer or the arrival of a specific date.
- The seller can require the intermediate party to either return the goods or transfer them to a third party (such as a different distributor or retailer).
- The intermediate party does not have an unconditional obligation to pay for the goods. This condition may still be the case, even if the party is required to pay a deposit to the seller.

EXAMPLE

Oberlin Acoustics has decided to accept the application of the Guitar Heaven retail chain to carry a selection of Oberlin electric guitars. However, Guitar Heaven does not have sufficient cash on hand to pay Oberlin within the customary 30-day terms. Instead, Oberlin agrees to an arrangement where Oberlin will be paid at once if Guitar Heaven sells one of its guitars, and will be paid in no later than 120 days, irrespective of any sales activity. If Oberlin receives an order from another customer for one of its guitars held in the Guitar Heaven inventory, it can direct Guitar Heaven to ship the guitar to the designated customer. This is essentially a consignment arrangement for the first 120 days, since Oberlin has control of the inventory for that period of time.

Thus, until the earlier of a sale to a third party or the passage of 120 days, Oberlin continues to record the guitars in its inventory, and does not recognize any revenue.

Customer Acceptance

A customer may include an acceptance clause in a contract with a seller. An acceptance clause states that the customer has the right to inspect goods and reject them or demand proper remedial efforts before formal acceptance. Normally, customer control over goods occurs as soon as this acceptance step has been completed.

There are situations in which the seller can determine that control has passed to a customer, even if a formal acceptance review has not yet taken place. This typically occurs when customer acceptance is based upon a delivery meeting very specific qualifications, such as certain dimension or weight requirements. If the seller can determine in advance that these criteria have been met, it can recognize revenue prior to formal customer acceptance. If the seller cannot determine in advance that a customer will accept the delivered goods, it must wait for formal acceptance before it can confirm that the customer had taken control of the delivery, which then triggers revenue recognition.

EXAMPLE

Stout Tanks, Inc. manufactures scuba tanks, which it sells in bulk to a large customer in Bonaire, Drive-Thru Scuba. Drive-Thru insists upon a complete hydrostatic test of each tank before accepting delivery, since an exploding air tank is a decidedly terminal experience for a diver wearing the tank. Stout decides to conducts its own hydrostatic test of every tank leaving its factory. Since Stout is conducting the same test as Drive-Thru, Stout can reasonably establish that customer acceptance has occurred as soon as the scuba tanks leave its factory. As such, Stout can recognize revenue on the delivery date, and not wait for Drive-Thru to conduct its test.

Even if a customer recognizes revenue in advance of formal customer acceptance, it may still be necessary to determine whether there are any remaining performance obligations to which a portion of the transaction price should be allocated. For example, a seller may have an obligation to not only manufacture production equipment, but also to install it at the customer site. This later step could be considered a separate performance obligation.

A variation on the customer acceptance concept is when a seller delivers goods to a customer for evaluation purposes. In this case, the customer has no obligation to accept or pay for the goods until the end of a trial period, so control cannot be said to have passed to the customer until such time as the customer accepts the goods or the trial period ends.

Customer Options for Additional Purchases

A seller may offer customers a number of ways in which to obtain additional goods or services at reduced rates or even for free. For example, the seller may offer a discount on a contract renewal, award points to frequent buyers, host periodic sales events, and so on.

When a contract grants a customer the right to acquire additional goods or services at a discount, this can be considered a performance obligation if the amount is material and the customer is essentially paying in advance for future goods or services. In this case, the seller recognizes revenue associated with the customer option when:

- The option expires; or
- The future goods or services are transferred to the customer.

If revenue is to be recognized for such an option, allocate the transaction price to the option based on the relative standalone price of the option. In the likely event that the standalone selling price of the option is not directly observable, use an estimate of its price. The derivation of this estimate should include the discount that the customer would obtain by exercising the option, adjusted for the following two items:

- Reduced by the amount of any discount that the customer could have received without the option, such as a standard ongoing discount offered to all customers; and
- The probability that the customer will not exercise the option.

A material right to additional purchases of goods or services is not considered to have been passed to a customer if the option is at a price that reflects the standalone selling price of a good or service. In this case, there is no particular advantage being granted to the customer, since it could just as easily purchase the goods or services at the same price, even in the absence of the option.

EXAMPLE

Twister Vacuum Company sells its top-of-the-line F5 vacuum cleaner to 50 customers for $800 each. As part of each sale, Twister gives each customer a discount code that, if used, gives the customer a 50% discount on the purchase of Twister's F1 hand-held vacuum cleaner, which normally sells for $100. The discount expires in 60 days.

In order to determine the standalone selling price of the discount code, Twister estimates (based on past experience) that 30% of all customers will use the code to purchase the F1 model. This means that the standalone selling price of the discount code is $15, which is calculated as follows:

$100 F1 standalone price × 50% discount × 30% probability of code usage = $15

The combined standalone selling prices of the F5 vacuum and the discount code sum to $815. Twister uses this information to allocate the $800 transaction price between the product and the discount code, using the following calculation:

Performance Obligation	Allocated Price	Calculation
F5 vacuum cleaner	$785.28	($800 ÷ $815) × $800
Discount code	14.72	($15 ÷ $815) × $800
Total	$800.00	

This allocation means that Twister can recognize $785.28 of revenue whenever it completes a performance obligation related to the sale of the F5 units to the 50 customers. Twister also allocates $14.72 to the discount code and recognizes the revenue associated with this item either when it is redeemed by a customer in the purchase of an F1 vacuum cleaner, or when the code expires.

EXAMPLE

Sojourn Hotel has a customer loyalty program that grants customers one loyalty point for each night that they stay in a Sojourn-affiliated hotel. Each loyalty point can be redeemed to reduce another stay at a Sojourn hotel by $5. If not used, the points expire after 24 months. During the most recent reporting period, customers earn 60,000 loyalty points on $2,000,000 of customer purchases. Based on past experience, Sojourn expects 60% of the points to be redeemed. Based on the likelihood of redemption, each point is worth $3 (calculated as $5 redemption value × 60% probability of redemption), so all of the points awarded are worth $180,000 (calculated as $3/ point × 60,000 points issued).

The loyalty points program gives a material right to customers that they would not otherwise have had if they had not stayed at a Sojourn hotel (i.e., entered into a contract with Sojourn). Thus, Sojourn concludes that the issued points constitute a performance obligation. Sojourn then allocates the $2,000,000 of customer purchases for hotel rooms to the hotel room product and the points awarded based on their standalone selling prices, based on the following calculations:

Performance Obligation	Allocated Price	Calculation
Hotel rooms	$1,834,862	($2,000,000 ÷ $2,180,000) × $2,000,000
Loyalty points	165,138	($180,000 ÷ $2,180,000) × $2,000,000
Total	$2,000,000	

The $165,138 allocated to loyalty points is initially recorded as a contract liability. The $1,834,862 allocated to hotel rooms is recognized as revenue, since Sojourn has completed its performance obligation related to these overnight stays.

As of the end of the next quarterly period, Sojourn finds that 8,000 of the loyalty points have been redeemed, so it recognizes revenue related to the loyalty points of $22,018 (calculated as 8,000 points ÷ 60,000 points × $165,138).

Donations

Topic 606 only applies to contracts with customers. What about goods or services received where there is no exchange between the two parties, as is the case when a nonprofit entity receives a donation? A donor may promise a nonprofit to contribute money to it in the future. This promise is called a *pledge*. There are many types of pledges, such as ones that are to be fulfilled all at one time, in increments, and with or without restrictions. The accounting for a pledge depends upon the conditions attached to it. The variations are:

- *Unconditional pledge.* When a donor commits to a pledge without reservation, the nonprofit receiving the funds records the pledge as revenue and an account receivable.
- *Conditional pledge.* When a donor commits to a pledge, but only when a condition is met, the nonprofit does not record anything. Instead, it waits for the condition to be fulfilled and then records the pledge as revenue and an account receivable. If the probability that a condition will *not* be fulfilled is remote, the pledge can be treated as an unconditional pledge.

EXAMPLE

Mole Industries has a standing policy of matching all donations made by its employees to Archimedes Education. The offer of Mole Industries is a conditional pledge, since it is contingent upon donations being made by its employees. In May, Mole's employees contribute $500 to Archimedes, so Mole pays Archimedes an additional $500. This matching amount can be recognized by Archimedes upon receipt.

EXAMPLE

The president of Mole Industries promises to give Archimedes an additional $10,000 donation if Archimedes provides him with its year-end financial statements. Since the probability that Archimedes will withhold this information is remote, Archimedes could treat the promise as an unconditional one, and recognize the revenue and an offsetting receivable at once.

When in doubt, a nonprofit should not record a pledge in the accounting records. Instead, wait for the situation to resolve itself, so that it can tell with certainty the circumstances under which a donor will make a contribution. In many cases, a simple notification of a forthcoming payment is not sufficient proof that a pledge exists. Instead, there should be a well-documented pledge that itemizes the amount to be paid and any conditions that must be fulfilled prior to payment.

If a pledge commitment is unconditional and legally enforceable, the nonprofit is required to recognize the present value of the entire series of payments. Present value is the current worth of the cash to be received in the future with one or more payments, which has been discounted at a market rate of interest.

The present value requirement is subject to the following variations:

- If the funds are to be received within one year, it is permissible to recognize the entire amount of the pledge, rather than just its present value.
- The estimated amount of cash flows can be used in the present value calculation, rather than the pledged amount. This allows management to be more conservative and recognize a lesser amount of revenue if it is uncertain about the total amount to be received or the timing of the receipt.

Tip: It is best to develop standardized pledge agreements for donors to sign, so that pledges can be recognized as revenue.

Gains and Losses from Nonfinancial Asset Derecognition

An organization may own nonfinancial assets, which it periodically derecognizes by selling or transferring to other entities. For example, a business could sell off used production equipment that it is no longer using. When this type of transaction takes place, the organization should recognize a gain or loss, rather than revenue. The gain or loss to be recognized is the difference between the consideration received and the carrying amount of the asset.

EXAMPLE

Mole Industries acquires a competitor that is in the same general markets, including the production of trench digging equipment and backhoes. However, the acquiree has also spent several years developing technology for digging pipeline bores through solid rock. Mole has assigned a fair value of $12,000,000 to this boring technology as part of its accounting for the business combination.

Mole is not interested in this technology, and sells it to Aquifers International, which drills tunnels for long-distance water transport. Aquifers has little excess cash, and so offers a minimal $2,000,000 payment in cash, plus 5% of all sales generated by the use of this technology for the next 10 years. Mole estimates that this 5% payment could result in a total payment of $20,000,000 over the 10-year period.

Mole's accountants conclude that the sale of this technology is not a good or service that Mole typically produces as part of its ordinary activities. Consequently, it is to be treated as the derecognition of a nonfinancial asset. Control has been passed to Aquifers, since the buyer can make immediate use of the related records and patents; Mole has retained no rights to the technology. The main issue is the nature of the consideration – it is not probable that the recognition of $20,000,000 of variable consideration will not eventually result in a significant reversal of this amount. The level of probability is especially difficult to discern, because the technology is entirely new, and so must be approved by a number of regulatory authorities before it can be used. Given the difficulty of generating sales from this technology, Mole elects to derecognize the asset and recognize a loss of $10,000,000, which is calculated as:

$2,000,000 cash payment – $12,000,000 carrying amount of asset
= $(10,000,000) derecognition loss

Mole's accountants will continue to reassess the transaction price in each successive year. If the circumstances ever change to the extent that it is no longer probable that a significant revenue reversal will *not* occur, additional variable consideration may be recognized.

Licensing

A seller may offer a license to use intellectual property owned by the seller. Examples of licensing arrangements are:

- Licensing to use software
- Licensing to listen to music
- Licensing to view a movie
- Franchising the name and processes of a restaurant
- Licensing of a book copyright to republish the book
- Licensing to use a patent within a product
- Licensing of a brand name, trade name, or logo

If a contract contains both a licensing agreement and a provision to provide goods or services to the customer, the seller must identify each performance obligation within the contract and allocate the transaction price to each one.

If the licensing agreement can be separated from the other elements of a contract, the seller must decide whether the license is being transferred to the customer over a period of time, or as of a point in time. A key point in making this determination is whether the license is intended to give the customer access to the intellectual property of the seller only as of the point in time when the license is granted, or over the duration of the license period. The first case would indicate that the revenue associated with the license is recognized as of a point in time, while the second case would indicate that the revenue is recognized over a period of time.

A license is more likely to have been granted as of a point in time when a customer can direct the use of a license and obtain substantially all of the remaining benefits from the license on the date when the license is granted to it. This will not be the case if the intellectual property to which the customer has rights continues to change throughout the license period, which occurs when the seller continues to engage in activities that significantly affect its intellectual property.

A seller's promise to provide a customer with a right to use its intellectual property is satisfied when the customer is able to use and benefit from the license. This is likely to be the case earlier when the intellectual property has significant standalone functionality, such as being able to perform a task or be aired. Examples of functional intellectual property are drug formulas, media content, and software.

The intent of the seller of a license is to provide the customer with the right to access its intellectual property when the seller commits to update the property, the customer will be exposed to the effects of those updates, and the updates do not result in the transfer of a good or service to the customer. These conditions may not be stated in a contract, but could be inferred from the seller's customary business practices. For example, if the customer pays the seller a royalty based on its sales of products derived from intellectual property provided by the seller, this implies that the seller will be updating the underlying intellectual property. If these conditions are present, the associated revenue should be recognized over time, rather than as of a point in time.

The seller may be granting a customer the right to use symbolic intellectual property, where the property does not have significant standalone functionality. Examples of symbolic intellectual property are brands, trade names, and logos. In this situation, the seller is likely continuing to support the intellectual property during the licensing period. Since the arrangement contains both a right of use and an implicit promise of ongoing support by the seller, this licensing arrangement is satisfied over a period of time. Therefore, revenue recognition should also occur over a period of time.

If the facts and circumstances of a contract indicate that the revenue associated with a contract should be recognized as of a point in time, this does not mean that the revenue can be recognized prior to the point in time when the customer can use and benefit from the license. This date may be later than the commencement date of the underlying contract. For example, the license to use intellectual property may be granted, but the actual property may not yet have been delivered to the customer or activated.

If it is not possible to separate the licensing agreement from the other components of a contract, account for them as a single performance obligation. An example of when this situation arises is when a license is integrated into a tangible product to such an extent that the product cannot be used without the license.

> **Note:** A guarantee by the seller that it will defend a patent from unauthorized use is not considered a performance obligation.

A contract under which there is a right to use a license may include the payment of a royalty to the seller. This arrangement may occur, for example, when the customer is acting as a distributor to re-sell the licensed intellectual property to other parties. In this situation, the seller may only recognize the royalty as revenue as of the later of these two events:

- The subsequent sale to or usage by the third party has occurred; or
- The underlying performance obligation associated with the royalty has been satisfied.

This royalty revenue accounting applies to a sales-based or usage-based royalty when the predominant item to which the royalty relates involves the licensing of intellectual property.

EXAMPLE

Territorial Lease Corporation (TLC) has spent years accumulating a massive database of oil and gas leases throughout the United States and Canada. It sells this information to oil and gas exploration companies, which use it to derive the prices at which they are willing to bid for oil and gas leases. TLC sells the information in three ways, which are:

- It sells a CD that contains lease information that is current as of the ship date. TLC does not issue any further updates to customers. Since TLC does not update the intellectual property, the associated revenue recognition can be considered to occur as of a point in time, which is the delivery date of the CD.
- The company also sells subscriptions to an on-line database of lease information, which it updates every day. Since TLC is continually upgrading the database, the recognition of revenue is considered to take place over time. Accordingly, TLC recognizes revenue over the term of the subscriptions it sells.
- TLC sells its lease information to another company, Enviro Consultants, which re-purposes the information for the environmental remediation industry. The information is billed to the customers of Enviro, and Enviro pays TLC a 50% royalty once Enviro receives payment from its customers. Since the subsequent sale of the information has occurred by the time TLC receives royalty payments, it can recognize the payments as revenue upon receipt.

Nonrefundable Upfront Fees

In some types of contracts, it is customary for the seller to charge a customer a nonre-fundable upfront fee. Examples of these fees are:

- Health club member ship fee
- Phone service activation fee
- Long-term contract setup fee

There may be a performance obligation associated with these fees. In some cases, it could actually relate to an activity that the seller completes at the beginning of a contract. However, this activity rarely relates to the fulfillment of a performance obligation by the seller, and simply represents an expenditure. Consequently, the most appropriate treatment of this fee is to recognize it as revenue when the goods or services stated in the contract are provided to the customer. Several additional issues to consider are:

- *Recognition period.* If the seller grants the customer a material option to renew the contract, the revenue recognition period associated with the upfront fee is extended over the additional contract term.
- *Setup costs.* It is possible that the costs incurred to set up a contract are an asset, which should be charged to expense over the course of the contract.

EXAMPLE

Providence Alarm Systems offers its customers a home monitoring system that includes a $200 setup fee and a monthly $35 charge to monitor their homes through an alarm system, for a minimum one-year period. Providence does not charge the setup fee again if a customer chooses to renew.

The setup activities that Providence engages in do not transfer a good or service to customers, and so do not create a performance obligation. Thus, the upfront fee can be considered an advance payment relating to the company's monthly monitoring activities. Providence should recognize the $200 fee over the initial one-year monitoring period, as services are provided.

Principal versus Agent

There are situations where the party providing goods or services to a customer is actually arranging to have another party provide the goods and services. In this case, the party is an agent, not the principal party acting as seller. Use the rules in the following exhibit to differentiate between the two concepts of principal and agent.

Principal vs. Agent Rules

Criterion	Principal	Agent
Controls the good or service before transfer to customer	Yes	No
Obtains legal title just prior to transfer to seller	Either	Either
Hires a subcontractor to fulfill some performance obligations	Yes	No
Arranges for the provision of goods or services by another party	No	Yes
Does not have inventory risk before or after the customer orders goods, including the absence of risk related to product returns	No	Yes
Does not have discretion in establishing prices	No	Yes
The consideration paid to the selling entity is in the form of a commission	No	Yes
There is no exposure to credit risk that the customer will not pay	No	Yes

The differentiation between principal and agent is of some importance, for a principal recognizes the gross amount of a sale, while an agent only recognizes the fee or commission it earns in exchange for its participation in the transaction. This fee or commission may be the net amount remaining after the agent has paid the principal the amount billed for its goods or services provided to the customer.

In a situation where the seller is initially the principal in a transaction but then hands off the performance obligation to a third party, the seller should not recognize the revenue associated with the performance obligation. Instead, the seller may have assumed the role of an agent.

A sale may include a number of components. If so, the party selling the goods or services should determine whether it is the principal or the agent for each item promised to the customer. It is possible that the seller could be the principal for some items and an agent for others, which means that the accounting treatment will vary for each one, as noted earlier in this section.

EXAMPLE

High Country Vacations operates a website that puts prospective vacationers in touch with resorts located in ski towns around the world. When a vacationer purchases a hotel room on the website, High Country takes a 15% commission from the resort where the hotel room is located. The resort sets the prices for hotel rooms. High Country is not responsible for the actual provision of hotel rooms to vacationers.

Since High Country does not control the hotel rooms being provided, is arranging for the provision of services by a third party, does not maintain an inventory of rooms, cannot establish prices, and is paid a commission, the company is clearly an agent in these transactions. Consequently, High Country should only recognize revenue in the amount of the commissions paid to it, not the amount paid by vacationers for their hotel rooms.

EXAMPLE

Dirt Cheap Tickets sells discounted tickets for cruises with several prominent cruise lines. The company purchases tickets in bulk from cruise lines and must pay for them, irrespective of its ability to re-sell the tickets to the public. Dirt Cheap can alter the prices of the tickets that it purchases, which typically means that the company gradually lowers prices as cruise dates approach, in order to ensure that its excess inventory of tickets is sold. There is no credit risk, since tickets are paid for at the point of purchase. If customers have issues with the cruise lines, Dirt Cheap will intercede on their behalf, but generally encourages them to go directly to the cruise lines with their complaints.

Based on its business model, Dirt Cheap is acting as the principal. It controls the goods being sold, has inventory risk, and actively alters prices. Consequently, Dirt Cheap can recognize revenue in the gross amount of the tickets sold.

Repurchase Agreements

A repurchase agreement is a contract in which the seller agrees to sell an asset and either promises or has the option to repurchase the asset. The asset that the seller repurchases can be the original asset sold, a substantially similar asset, or an asset of which the original unit is a part. There are three variations on the repurchase agreement:

- *Forward.* The seller has an obligation to repurchase the asset.
- *Call option.* The seller has the right to repurchase the asset.

- *Put option*. The seller has an obligation to repurchase the asset if required to by the customer.

If the contract is essentially a forward or call option, the customer never gains control of the asset, since the seller can or will take it back. Given the circumstances, revenue recognition can vary as follows:

- *Reduced repurchase price*. If the seller either can or must repurchase the asset for an amount less than the original selling price (considering the time value of money), the seller accounts for the transaction as a lease.
- *Same or higher repurchase price*. If the seller either can or must repurchase the asset for an amount equal to or greater than the original selling price (considering the time value of money), the seller accounts for the transaction as a financing arrangement.
- *Sale-leaseback*. If the transaction is a sale-leaseback arrangement, the seller accounts for the transaction as a financing arrangement.

When a customer has a put option, the proper accounting depends upon the market price of the asset and the existence of a sale-leaseback arrangement. The alternatives are:

- *Incentive to exercise option*. If the customer has a significant economic incentive to exercise the option, the seller accounts for the transaction as a lease. Such an incentive would exist, for example, when the repurchase price exceeds the expected market value of an asset through the period when the put option can be exercised (considering the time value of money).
- *No incentive to exercise option*. If the customer does not have an economic incentive to exercise a put option, the seller accounts for the agreement as a sale of a product with a right of return.
- *Sale-leaseback*. Even if the seller has a significant economic incentive, as noted in the last bullet point, if the arrangement is a sale-leaseback arrangement, the seller accounts for it as a financing arrangement.
- *Higher repurchase price*. If the repurchase price is equal to or higher than the selling price and is more than the asset's expected market value (considering the time value of money), the seller accounts for it as a financing arrangement.
- *Higher repurchase price with no incentive*. In the rare case where the repurchase price is equal to or higher than the original purchase price, but is less than or equal to the expected market value of the asset (considering the time value of money), this indicates that the customer has no economic incentive to exercise the option. In this case, the seller accounts for the transaction as a sale of a product with a right of return.

When the seller accounts for a transaction as a financing arrangement, the seller continues to recognize the asset, as well as a liability for any consideration it has received from the customer. The difference between the amount of consideration paid by and due to the customer is to be recognized as interest and processing (or related) costs.

If a call option or put option expires without being exercised, the seller can derecognize the repurchase liability and recognize revenue instead.

EXAMPLE

Domicilio Corporation sells a commercial property to Mole Industries for $3,000,000 on March 1, but retains the right to repurchase the property for $3,050,000 on or before December 31 of the same year. This transaction is a call option.

Control over the property does not pass to Mole Industries until after the December 31 termination date of the call option, since Domicilio can repurchase the asset. In the meantime, Domicilio accounts for the arrangement as a financing transaction, since the exercise price exceeds the amount of Mole's purchase price. This means that Domicilio retains the asset in its accounting records, records the $3,000,000 of cash received as a liability, and recognizes interest expense of $50,000 over the intervening months, which gradually increases the amount of the liability to $3,050,000.

On December 31, Domicilio lets the call option lapse; it can now derecognize the liability and recognize $3,050,000 of revenue.

EXAMPLE

Assume the same transaction, except that the option is a requirement for Domicilio to repurchase the property for $2,900,000 at the behest of the customer, Mole Industries. This is a put option. The market value by the end of the year is expected to be lower than $2,900,000.

At the inception of the contract, it is apparent that Mole will have an economic incentive to exercise the put option, since it can earn more from exercising the option than from retaining the property. This means that control over the property does not really pass to Mole. In essence, then, the transaction is to be considered a lease.

Share-Based Payments to Customers

A seller may grant share-based payments to a customer as part of a sale transaction. If so, the amount recorded is a reduction of the transaction price, and is measured on the basis of the fair value of the award as of the grant date. The grant date is the date on which the two parties reach a mutual understanding of the key terms and conditions of the payment award.

If the number of equity instruments promised in a contract is variable due to a service condition or a performance condition that affects the vesting of an award, the seller should estimate the number of equity instruments that it will be obligated to issue to its customer and update the estimate of the number of equity instruments until the award ultimately vests.

Unexercised Rights of Customers

A customer may prepay for goods or services to be delivered at a later date, which the seller initially records as a liability, and later as revenue when the goods or services are delivered. However, what if the customer does not exercise all of its rights to have goods or services delivered? The unexercised amount of this prepayment may be referred to as *breakage*.

The amount of breakage associated with a customer prepayment should be recognized as revenue. The question is, when should the recognition occur? There are two possible scenarios:

- *Existing pattern.* If there is a historical pattern of how a customer exercises the rights associated with its prepayments, the seller can estimate the amount of breakage likely to occur, and recognize it in proportion to the pattern of rights exercised by the customer.
- *No expectation.* If there is no expectation that the seller will be entitled to any breakage, the seller recognizes revenue associated with breakage only when there is a remote likelihood that the customer will exercise any remaining rights.

No revenue related to breakage should be recognized if it is probable that such recognition will result in a significant revenue reversal at a later date.

In a situation where there are unclaimed property laws, the seller is legally required to remit breakage to the applicable government entity. In this case, the breakage is recorded as a liability (rather than revenue), which is cleared from the seller's books when the funds are remitted to the government.

EXAMPLE

Clyde Shotguns receives a $10,000 deposit from a customer, to be used for the construction of a custom-made shotgun. Clyde completes the weapon and delivers it to the customer, recognizing $9,800 of revenue based on the number of billable hours expended. Clyde notifies the customer of the residual deposit amount, but the customer does not respond, despite repeated attempts at communication. Under the escheatment laws of the local state government, Clyde is required to remit these residual funds to the state if they have not been claimed within three years. Accordingly, Clyde initially records the $200 as an escheatment liability, and pays over the funds to the government once three years have passed.

Warranties

A warranty is a guarantee related to the performance of delivered goods or services. If related to a product, the seller typically guarantees the replacement or repair of the delivered goods. If related to a service, the warranty may involve replacement services, or a full or partial refund.

If a customer has the option to separately purchase a warranty, this is to be considered a distinct service to be provided by the seller. As such, the warranty is to be considered a separate performance obligation, with a portion of the transaction price allocated to it. If there is no option for the customer to separately purchase a warranty, the warranty is instead considered an obligation of the seller, in which case the following accounting applies:

- Accrue a reserve for product warranty claims based on the prior experience of the business. In the absence of such experience, the company can instead rely upon the experience of other entities in the same industry. If there is considerable uncertainty in regard to the amount of projected product warranties, it may not be possible to record a product sale until the warranty period has expired or more experience has been gained with customer claims.
- Adjust the reserve over time to reflect changes in prior and expected experience with warranty claims. This can involve a credit to earnings if the amount of the reserve is too large, and should be reduced.
- If there is a history of minimal warranty expenditures, there is no need to accrue a reserve for product warranty claims.

A warranty may provide a customer with a service, as well as a guarantee that provided goods or services will function as claimed. Consider the following items when determining whether a service exists:

- *Duration*. The time period needed to discover whether goods or services are faulty is relatively short, so a long warranty period is indicative of an additional service being offered.
- *Legal requirement*. There is a legal requirement to provide a warranty, in which case the seller is more likely to just be offering the mandated warranty without an additional service.
- *Tasks*. If the warranty requires the seller to perform specific tasks that are identifiable with the remediation of faulty goods or services, there is unlikely to be any additional identifiable service being offered.

If an additional service is being offered through a warranty, consider this service to be a performance obligation, and allocate a portion of the transaction price to that service. If the seller cannot reasonably account for this service separately, instead account for both the assurance and service aspects of the warranty as a bundled performance obligation.

There may be a legal obligation for the seller to compensate its customers if its goods or services cause harm. If so, this is not considered a performance obligation. Instead, this legal obligation is considered a loss contingency. A loss contingency arises when there is a situation for which the outcome is uncertain, and which should be resolved in the future, possibly creating a loss. For example, there may be injuries caused by a company's products when it is discovered that lead-based paint has been used on toys sold by the business.

When deciding whether to account for a loss contingency, the basic concept is to only record a loss that is probable, and for which the amount of the loss can be reasonably estimated. If the best estimate of the amount of the loss is within a range, accrue whichever amount appears to be a better estimate than the other estimates in the range. If there is no "better estimate" in the range, accrue a loss for the minimum amount in the range.

If it is not possible to arrive at a reasonable estimate of the loss associated with an event, only disclose the existence of the contingency in the notes accompanying the financial statements. Or, if it is not probable that a loss will be incurred, even if it is possible to estimate the amount of a loss, only disclose the circumstances of the contingency without accruing a loss.

If the conditions for recording a loss contingency are initially not met, but then *are* met during a later accounting period, the loss should be accrued in the later period. Do not make a retroactive adjustment to an earlier period to record a loss contingency.

Summary

Though the topics addressed in this chapter might be considered special revenue recognition situations, the underlying principles upon which their accounting is based are derived straight from the recognition principles outlined in the first chapter. This means that the correct accounting is based on when control passes to the customer, whether there is a separate performance obligation, and whether the performance obligation is completed as of a point in time or over time. These themes are present throughout the topics covered in this chapter. In essence, the accounting standards have been formulated to adhere to the same principles in as many cases as possible, to prevent unorthodox accounting solutions.

Chapter 3
Revenue Presentation and Disclosure

Introduction

How should revenue-related information be presented in the financial statements and the accompanying footnotes? The following section notes the proper presentation of contract assets and liabilities, product return information, and impairments in the financial statements. The more extensive Disclosures section addresses the detailed revenue reporting requirements that should appear in the notes accompanying the financial statements.

Presentation

When there is performance under a contract, this can give rise to a contract asset or liability. A contract asset arises when an organization has performed more under a contract than it has yet received in customer payments. If there is an unconditional right to be paid (i.e., only the passage of time is needed before payment is due), the seller should separately present this amount in the balance sheet as an account receivable. When there is a receivable, this reduces the presented amount of any remaining contract asset. In effect, elements of the contract asset are now being presented as part of the accounts receivable line item and the contract asset line item.

Conversely, a contract liability arises when an organization has been paid more by the customer than it has yet performed under a contract. This liability is to be presented within a separate line item in the balance sheet.

If there are impairment losses associated with contract assets, they should appear in the income statement.

If the seller is recording a liability for projected product returns and an asset for the right to recovered products under sales return arrangements, do not net the two together into a single line item. Each is to be presented separately.

Disclosures

There are a number of disclosures related to revenue. As a general overview, the intent of the disclosures is to reveal enough information so that readers will understand the nature of the revenue, the amount being recognized, the timing associated with its recognition, and the uncertainty of the related cash flows. More specifically, disclosures are required in the following three areas for both annual and interim financial statements:

- *Contracts*. Disclose the amount of revenue recognized, any revenue impairments, the disaggregation of revenue, performance obligations, contract balances, and the amount of the transaction price allocated to the remaining performance obligations. Contract balances should include beginning and ending balances of receivables, contract assets, and contract liabilities. In particular:

- o *Revenue.* Separately disclose the revenue recognized from contracts with customers.
- o *Impairment losses.* Separately disclose any impairment losses on receivables or contract assets that arose from contracts with customers. These disclosures must be separated from the disclosure of losses from other types of contracts.
- o *Disaggregation.* Disaggregate the reported amount of revenue recognized into categories that reflect the nature, amount, timing, and uncertainty of cash flows and revenue. Examples are:
  - By contract type (such as by cost-plus versus fixed-price contract)
  - By country or region
  - By customer type (such as by retail versus government customer)
  - By duration of contract
  - By major product line
  - By market
  - By sales channels (such as by Internet store, retail chain, or wholesaler)
  - By transfer timing (such as sales as of a point in time versus over time)

  The nature of this disaggregation may be derived from how the organization discloses information about revenue in other venues, such as within annual reports, in presentations to investors, or when being evaluated for financial performance or resource allocation judgments. If the entity is publicly-held and therefore reports segment information, consider how the reporting of disaggregated revenue information might relate to the revenue information reported for segments of the business. It is also allowable for certain non-public entities to *not* disaggregate revenue information, but only if this disclosure is replaced by the disclosure of revenue by the timing of transfers to customers, and with a discussion of how economic factors (such as contract types or customer types) impact the nature, amount, timing, and uncertainty of cash flows and revenue.

EXAMPLE

Lowry Locomotion operates a number of business segments generally related to different types of trains. It compiles the following information for its disaggregation disclosure:

(000s) Segments	Freight Trains	Passenger Trains	Railbus	Total
Primary Geographical Markets				
Europe	$53,000	$41,000	$14,000	$108,000
North America	91,000	190,000	---	281,000
	$144,000	$231,000	$14,000	$389,000
Major Product Lines				
Diesel	$106,000	$---	$---	$106,000
Electric	38,000	190,000	14,000	242,000
Trolleys	---	41,000	---	41,000
	$144,000	$231,000	$14,000	$389,000
Timing of Revenue Recognition				
Goods transferred at a point in time	$129,000	$189,000	$11,000	$329,000
Services transferred over time	15,000	42,000	3,000	60,000
	$144,000	$231,000	$14,000	$389,000

- o *Contract-related.* The disclosure of contract balances for all entities shall include the opening and closing balances of receivables, contract assets, and contract liabilities. Publicly-held and certain other entities must provide considerably more information. This includes:
  - Revenue recognized in the period that was included in the contract liability at the beginning of the period, and revenue recognized in the period from performance obligations at least partially satisfied in previous periods (such as from changes in transaction prices).
  - How the timing of the completion of performance obligations relates to the timing of payments from customers and the impact this has on the balances of contract assets and contract liabilities.
  - Explain significant changes in the balances of contract assets and contract liabilities in the period. Possible causes to discuss might include changes caused by business combinations, impairments, or cumulative catch-up adjustments.
- o *Performance obligations.* Describe the performance obligations related to contracts with customers, which should include the timing of when these obligations are typically satisfied (such as upon delivery), significant payment terms, the presence of any significant financing components, whether consideration is variable, and whether the

consideration may be constrained. Also note the nature of the goods or services being transferred, and describe any obligations to have a third party transfer goods or services to customers (as is the case in an agent relationship). Finally, describe any obligations related to returns, refunds, and warranties.

- o *Price allocations.* If there are remaining performance obligations to which transaction prices are to be allocated, disclose the aggregate transaction price allocated to those unsatisfied obligations. Also note when this remaining revenue is likely to be recognized, either in a qualitative discussion or by breaking down the amounts to be recognized by time band. None of these disclosures are needed if the original expected duration of a contract's performance obligation is for less than one year. Also, certain non-public entities can elect to not disclose any of this information.

It is possible to not disclose the preceding information for variable consideration when the consideration is a sales-based or usage-based royalty that is being paid in exchange for an intellectual property license, or when the consideration is allocated to a wholly unsatisfied performance obligation. However, doing so requires the entity to describe the nature of the consideration that has not be disclosed.

EXAMPLE

Franklin Oilfield Support provides gas field maintenance to gas exploration companies in North America. Franklin discloses the following information related to the allocation of transaction prices to remaining performance obligations:

Franklin provides gas field maintenance services to several of the larger gas exploration firms in the Bakken field in North Dakota. The company typically enters into two-year maintenance service agreements. Currently, the remaining performance obligations are for $77,485,000, which are expected to be satisfied within the next 24 months. These obligations are noted in the following table, which also states the year in which revenue recognition is expected:

(000s)	20X1	20X2	Totals
Revenue expected to be recognized:			
Gates contract	$14,250	$7,090	$21,340
Hollander contract	23,825	17,900	41,725
Ives contract	9,070	5,350	14,420
Totals	$47,145	$30,340	$77,485

- *Judgments.* Note the timing associated with when performance obligations are satisfied, as well as how the transaction price was determined and how it was allocated to the various performance obligations. In particular:

- o *Recognition methods.* When performance obligations are to be satisfied over time, describe the methods used to recognize revenue, and explain why these methods constitute a faithful depiction of the transfer of goods or services to customers.
- o *Transfer of control.* When performance obligations are satisfied as of a point in time, disclose the judgments made to determine when a customer gains control of the goods or services promised under contracts.
- o *Methods, inputs and assumptions.* Disclose sufficient information about the methods, inputs, and assumptions used to determine transaction prices, the constraints on any variable consideration, allocation of transaction prices, and measurement of obligations for returns, refunds, and so forth. The discussion of transaction prices should include how variable consideration is estimated, how noncash consideration is measured, and how the time value of money is used to adjust prices.
- o *Disclosure avoidance.* Certain non-public entities can elect not to disclose information about the following items pertaining to judgments:

  - Why revenue recognition methods constitute a faithful depiction of the transfer of goods or services to customers.
  - The judgments made to determine when a customer gains control of the goods or services promised under contracts.
  - All methods, inputs, and assumptions used, though this information must still be supplied in regard to the determination of whether variable consideration is constrained.

- *Asset recognition.* Note the recognized assets associated with obtaining or completing the terms of the contract. This shall include the closing balances of contract-related assets by main category of asset, such as for setup costs and the costs to obtain contracts. The disclosure should also include the amount of amortization expenses and impairment losses recognized in the period. Also describe:

  - o *Judgments.* The judgments involved in determining the amount of costs incurred to obtain or fulfill a customer contract.
  - o *Amortization.* The amortization method used to charge contract-related costs to expense in each reporting period.

A non-public entity can elect not to make the disclosures just noted for asset recognition.

It may be necessary to aggregate or disaggregate these disclosures to clarify the information presented. In particular, do not obscure information by adding large amounts of insignificant detail, or by combining items whose characteristics are substantially different.

There may be a change in estimate related to the measurement of progress toward completion of a performance obligation. If the change in estimate will affect several future periods, disclose the effect on income from continuing operations, net income, and any related per-share amounts (if the entity is publicly held). This disclosure is only required if the change is material. If there is not an immediate material effect, but a material effect is expected in later periods, provide a description of the change in estimate.

Summary

A key point to search for in the enumeration of revenue disclosures is that many of them do not apply to privately-held entities. All of them apply to publicly-held entities, but in many cases a privately-held organization can elect to either dispense with certain disclosures, or replace them with lesser summary-level descriptions. This difference in disclosure requirements was enacted in order to reduce the disclosure labor for privately-held organizations, while still providing full disclosures for the needs of investors in publicly-held businesses.

Chapter 4
Management of Revenue Recognition

Introduction

Thus far, we have been engaged in an enumeration of the many requirements placed on revenue recognition by GAAP, and in providing explanatory examples. But what about the *management* of revenue recognition? Are there more efficient ways to recognize revenue? In this chapter, we depart from accounting requirements, and instead provide advice regarding the day-to-day handling of revenue recognition transactions. The following topics are presented in the order in which the related accounting requirements were stated in the preceding chapters.

Identification of Customers

Revenue can only be recognized if the seller is engaged in transactions with a customer. This may seem painfully obvious, and yet it is quite possible that there are transactions going on with entities that are *not* customers. If so, and the seller has been routinely recording revenue from these transactions for years, it may come as quite a shock when the auditors delve into these relationships and declare that some counterparties are not customers at all, and that all associated revenue must be removed from the books.

This problem is most likely to arise for those customers located on the periphery of the seller's business activities, where there is some other transaction occurring that does not involve the transfer of goods or services. These transactions may have been going on for so long that it has never occurred to anyone in the accounting department to question them.

To guard against the mis-identification of third parties as customers, consider implementing one or more of the following items:

- *Internal audit examination.* Ask the internal audit manager to schedule an audit that is specifically targeted at the nature of the seller's customers. This could result in recommendations to make systemic changes that can more easily spot non-customer relationships in the future.
- *Senior-level review.* Have the CFO and controller mutually review any existing relationships that do not involve the normal transfer of goods or services.
- *In-process review.* Require a senior staff person to review the nature of each proposed sale transaction to see if the counterparty can be classified as a customer. This approach may not work well if there are many new customers to be sorted through, or if there is not sufficient staff time to conduct a detailed review.

Contractual Consistency

Much of the revenue recognition standard revolves around the existence of a contract, the performance obligations stated in the contract, and the pricing stated in the contract. The job of the accountant is made vastly more difficult if it is hard to determine whether a contract exists, or if there are non-standard elements in the contract relating to performance obligations and pricing. Consequently, the emphasis on contracts makes it more important than ever to insist on the use of standardized contract terms.

It may not be wise to force customers into a completely regimented contractual arrangement that allows for no variation, especially if doing so will repel customers or interfere with the corporate sales strategy. Nonetheless, the controller and CFO should vigorously point out the ramifications on revenue recognition of continually altering contracts. Not only does this require more accounting staff time for contract examinations, but it will also necessitate more time by the company's auditors to review contracts, which will increase the price of the audit.

One way to deal with customer demands for variances from contracts is to derive a small number of standard contracts, each one incorporating a different set of features designed to appeal to a certain set of customer requirements. The accounting staff can then develop a procedure for how to account for each contract type, so that the work associated with the extra contract variations is minimized. This approach may work well for customers, who can now at least have some of their demands met by switching to a different contract format.

Another option is to provide the sales staff with a list of which contract features can be changed without altering the underlying revenue recognition. It is permissible to negotiate with customers over these items. There should also be another list of contract topics that cannot be changed without supervisory approval, since they *will* alter the revenue recognition (such as a clause allowing a customer to cancel a contract without paying).

Contract Aggregation

If the seller deals with large numbers of contracts on a regular basis, it can make sense from an efficiency perspective to formally aggregate these contracts for revenue recognition purposes. Then the accounting staff does not have to conduct a separate review of each contract. To make aggregation a viable option, all contracts in an aggregated group must have essentially the same terms, which leads us back to the contract consistency recommendations noted in the last section.

Performance Clarification

Revenue recognition is closely tied to the identification of performance obligations. If the wording of such an obligation is excessively vague, the auditors may take a conservative stance and aggregate the obligation with other obligations in a contract; doing so could delay revenue recognition. To keep this from happening, review the line items in recent contracts to see if the wording can be more precisely defined to state exactly which goods are to be shipped or services performed. The result may be a higher level of regimentation in the construction of contracts, either to ensure that certain stock phrases are used to describe performance obligations, or to employ more robust contract reviews before they are issued to customers.

Another variation on the concept of performance clarification is to install a feedback loop, so that any problems found with existing contracts are examined and remedial action taken to ensure that the same problems do not arise in future contracts.

Variable Consideration Analysis

One of the most time-consuming aspects of revenue recognition is the examination of a contract to find any variable consideration elements, and then deciding how much to recognize as revenue. This may require an inordinate amount of staff time in each reporting period, and is also subject to pressure from management to emphasize more optimistic results. Here are several ways to deal with the situation:

- *Only review at longer intervals.* If the financial statements are only being generated for internal use, do not bother with ongoing reviews of variable consideration arrangements. Instead, review at longer intervals, such as on a quarterly or even an annual basis. A publicly-held business, which must release quarterly results, will likely require a quarterly review of variable consideration. A privately-held entity may consider it sufficient to only conduct this review at the end of its fiscal year.
- *Standardize the methodology.* Even though the accounting standard allows for the use of multiple methods to derive the amount of consideration most likely to be paid, try to centralize on just one method. By doing so, the accounting staff can come up with a well-documented and tightly regimented approach that can be reliably applied to many situations.
- *Audit material changes.* If there is pressure from senior management to give an optimistic spin to the amount of variable consideration, have the internal audit staff review the documentation pertaining to all variable consideration decisions. If this group finds evidence of fraud, they can bring it to the attention of the audit committee, which reports to the board of directors – not senior management.

Time Value of Money Analysis

If the transaction price is to be paid over a lengthy period of time, it is likely that the accounting staff will be required to break out a financing component in the recognition of revenue. There may be no way to avoid the offending payment terms that trigger the need for a time value of money analysis. If this is the case, and these types of contracts are fairly common, consider constructing a standard procedure that deals with the following issues:

- Precisely defines which contract types are most likely to contain a financing component.

- Regiments the process of determining the discount rate that should be applied to each transaction. Consider having the company's auditors approve this part of the procedure in advance, so there will be no reason to alter discount rates after the audit has begun.
- Gives examples of the journal entries to be used, with examples. Also construct journal entry templates that can be used to create these entries, thereby reducing the risk of error.

In general, an organization will want to avoid recording a financing component, not only because of the extra accounting labor involved, but also because doing so shifts some revenue into interest income; this reduces the amount of revenue from operations that an entity can report. One way to mitigate the effects of the time value of money on contracts is to conduct a formal review of those situations in which a financing component may be called for, and formally document any reasons why management believes that the time value of money is not relevant. If these reasons are adequate, the auditors may approve of situations in which the recognition of interest income can be avoided.

Standalone Selling Prices

The allocation of prices to performance obligations is based on the standalone selling prices of the seller's goods and services. This can be a difficult chore if the seller does not actually sell these items separately. If so, a poorly-organized accounting staff might find itself wasting an inordinate amount of time justifying the allocation of prices to each element of a large number of contracts.

A better approach is to develop a formal justification for the standalone selling price of each good or service that the seller offers, based upon all relevant information, such as product costs, profit margins, the seller's pricing strategy, competitor pricing, and so forth. This document is then used to allocate prices for all relevant contracts, possibly with some adjustment for the unique circumstances of each contract. This formal justification document will likely require revision at regular intervals, so assign a version number to each replacement document, and have a procedure in place to ensure that all targeted recipients replace the old version with the new version. It will also be necessary to retain *all* versions, to justify the seller's pricing to the auditors.

Measurement of Progress Completion

A seller might be tempted to create an elaborate new system to measure its progress toward completing various performance obligations under a contract. However, any new measurement system imposes an administrative cost, especially if it is in addition to existing measurement systems. Consequently, it can be better to continue using an existing progress measurement system, unless its results are significantly altering revenue recognition from what it should be.

If management is contemplating a change to a new measurement system, it would be both useful and cost-effective to first use the new system on a pilot basis to determine its impact on revenue recognition. The results could be shared with the auditors to see if they agree with the new system, and then incorporate any necessary revisions into the system before rolling it out throughout the business. Otherwise, management may be startled to find that its recognized revenue levels are unusually high, low, or variable in relation to the previous situation.

Costs to Obtain a Contract

The criteria noted in the accounting standard for the capitalization of costs to obtain a contract are highly specific; in most cases, all costs incurred to obtain a contract will likely need to be charged to expense as incurred. The one case in which a cost could be capitalized is when a commission payment is triggered by a contract award.

We suggest that it is not efficient from an accounting perspective to capitalize the cost of commissions, since the accounting staff must continually monitor these amounts and amortize them over the contract period. Instead, unless the commission is quite large, the easier approach will likely be to charge commissions to expense as incurred. Alternatively, alter the commission arrangement so that these payments are earned as performance obligations are fulfilled; doing so shifts the expense recognition further into the future and more closely matches the expense to the associated revenue.

Bill-and-Hold Arrangements

Bill-and-hold arrangements have historically been viewed by auditors with deep suspicion, since they frequently mask instances where the seller is really trying to bolster its recognized revenue despite being unable to ship goods. Though bill-and-hold transactions are still allowed, they continue to be situated at the outer fringes of allowable revenue transactions. Consequently, it could be useful to adopt a formal policy of never recording such transactions. Doing so also avoids the extra labor required to split out the custodial function from the amount of revenue to be recognized.

Breakage

There may be instances where a seller will experience breakage, which is the unexercised amount of a customer prepayment. It is theoretically possible that the seller could recognize breakage as revenue. However, it is far more likely that the local government will demand that these funds be forwarded to it under escheatment laws. Given the likelihood of the latter situation, it is easier to not deal with the potential revenue recognition aspects of breakage, and instead assume that these funds will become a liability of the seller until such time as they are forwarded to the government.

Summary

As noted in the introduction, the suggestions in this chapter have focused on improving the efficiency of handling revenue recognition issues. An underlying theme of the chapter has been that increased efficiency typically comes from standardization. This means that contracts should be structured in the same way and contain nearly the same text for all sales transactions. The effort required to recognize revenue increases greatly as soon as the seller engages in customized transactions; also, these more customized arrangements are more likely to have variable interpretations regarding when revenue should be recognized, and in what amounts.

Glossary

A

Agent. A person or entity acting on behalf of another.

B

Bill-and-hold. Where the seller retains goods on behalf of the customer, but still recognizes revenue.

Breakage. That portion of a customer advance payment that is never used by the customer.

C

Change in accounting estimate. A change that adjusts the carrying amount of an asset or liability, or the subsequent accounting for it.

Consideration. Something of monetary value paid to a third party in exchange for goods, services, or other benefits.

Consignment. When the owner of goods delivers them to an intermediary, who holds them for sale to the end customer. The owner retains control of the goods while waiting for the final sale transaction.

Contract. An agreement between at least two parties that creates enforceable obligations and rights.

Contract asset. The seller's right to consideration in exchange for goods or services.

Contract liability. The seller's obligation to transfer goods or services to a customer, which is paying consideration to the seller in exchange.

Contract modification. A scope or price alteration of a contract that is approved by both parties to the contract.

Customer. An entity that has contracted to obtain goods or services from the seller's ordinary activities in exchange for payment.

P

Performance obligation. A contractual obligation to transfer a good or service to a customer.

Pledge. A promise by a donor to make a contribution on a future date.

Principal. The main party to a transaction.

Publicly held entity. An entity that is required to issue financial statements to the Securities and Exchange Commission or a foreign regulatory agency.

R

Revenue. An asset enhancement or liability settlement caused by the delivery of goods or services that comprise an entity's central operations.

S

Standalone selling price. That price at which a good or service can be sold by itself in a separate transaction.

T

Transaction price. The consideration to be paid by a customer in exchange for its receipt of goods or services.

Index

www.ingramcontent.com/pod-product-compliance
Lightning Source LLC
Chambersburg PA
CBHW051420200326
41520CB00023B/7312